D1617265

Gadamer's Ethics of Play

Gadamer's Ethics of Play

Hermeneutics and the Other

Monica Vilhauer

LEXINGTON BOOKS
A division of
ROWMAN & LITTLEFIELD PUBLISHERS, INC.
Lanham • Boulder • New York • Toronto • Plymouth, UK

Published by Lexington Books
A division of Rowman & Littlefield Publishers, Inc.
A wholly owned subsidiary of The Rowman & Littlefield Publishing Group, Inc.
4501 Forbes Boulevard, Suite 200, Lanham, Maryland 20706
http://www.lexingtonbooks.com

Estover Road, Plymouth PL6 7PY, United Kingdom

British Library Cataloguing in Publication Information Available

Library of Congress Cataloging-in-Publication Data
Vilhauer, Monica.
 Gadamer's ethics of play : hermeneutics and the other / Monica Vilhauer.
   p. cm.
 Includes bibliographical references (p.   ) and index.
 ISBN 978-0-7391-3914-1 (cloth : alk. paper) — ISBN 978-0-7391-3916-5
(electronic)
 1. Gadamer, Hans-Georg, 1900–2002. Wahrheit und Methode. 2. Hermeneutics.
3. Play (Philosophy) 4. Other (Philosophy) 5. Ethics. I. Title.
 B3248.G33W34375 2010
 175—dc22   2010022960

⊖™ The paper used in this publication meets the minimum requirements of
American National Standard for Information Sciences—Permanence of Paper for
Printed Library Materials, ANSI/NISO Z39.48-1992.

Printed in the United States of America

To my parents,
lifelong dialogue partners

Contents

Acknowledgments

This project has gone through a number of stages on the way to its final form as a book. I'd like to offer my thanks to a number of teachers, colleagues, and friends who have supported the life of this work as it has developed.

First, I offer great thanks to those teachers who nurtured and critiqued my early work on Gadamer at the New School for Social Research. My special thanks go to Richard Bernstein, who introduced me to Gadamer and offered me much needed encouragement while I was writing a first version of this book. His enthusiasm in the classroom, and his special ability to recognize, and hold in check, all signs of sophistry, continues to inspire me in my thinking and in my own teaching. I also want to offer special thanks to Alice Crary and Dmitri Nikulin for their thoughtful feedback on my early draft of the present work, and their willingness to offer guidance any time I needed it.

Second, I am grateful to my colleagues in the Religion and Philosophy Department at Roanoke College, who have so kindly offered their friendship and advice to me as I have attempted to learn how to juggle the three balls of teaching, research, and service. My thanks go to Brent Adkins, Jennifer Berenson, Paul Hinlicky, Marwood Larson-Harris, Gerry McDermott, Eric Rothgery, Ned Wisnefske, and Hans Zorn. I am so thankful for their collective wisdom, and the openness with which they have welcomed me into the department. I am also grateful to Roanoke College for the Faculty Scholar Award, which offered me the time necessary to complete my manuscript and prepare it for publication.

Third, there is a special group of friends out there that has been willing to brainstorm with me, strategize with me, and read and respond to my writing as the long process of this project has come to a close. I am indebted to these people for their thoughtfulness, time, and conversation. Thank you to Jake Vilhauer, Brent Adkins, Lauren Swayne Barthold, and Rachel Neithercut for helping me to reach the finish line!

I presented many of the ideas from chapter 3 to the Graduate Faculty Women in Philosophy group at the New School for Social Research in 2004, and am thankful for the thoughtful feedback of that group. I also want to thank the editors of the *Women in Philosophy* journal of the New School for Social Research for the permission to revise and use my article "Understanding the Play Structure of Understanding: The Model of Art," from the 2004–2005 volume of the *WIP* journal, in this book. I presented many of the ideas from chapter 6 to the XVIth International Symposium of the Olympic Center for Philosophy and Culture in 2005, and benefited from conversations with participants of the symposium. I thank the editor of *Skepsis* for the permission to revise and use parts of my article "Socratic Dialogue and the Ethical Conditions of Knowledge," from *Skepsis* volume 26:1–2, 2005, in this book. I presented ideas from chapters 3, 4, and 5 at the Eastern Division meeting of the American Philosophical Association in 2008, and the Society for Phenomenology and Existential Philosophy meeting in 2008. I am thankful for the insightful questions and comments offered by participants at both meetings, especially those of Lauren Swayne Barthold, who commented on my paper at the Eastern APA meeting. I thank David Pellauer, editor of *Philosophy Today*, for permission to include portions of my SPEP paper in this book, which appeared in volume 53:4 (Winter 2009) of *Philosophy Today* under the title "Beyond the 'Fusion of Horizons': Gadamer's Notion of Understanding as 'Play.'" Finally, I appreciate the permission that Continuum International Publishing Group has offered me to publish portions of *Truth and Method* in this book.

I want to thank, also, an anonymous reviewer enlisted by Lexington Books, whose careful reading of the manuscript and tough criticism has pushed me to make the book better.

I am grateful to Jeff Hofmann for creating the cover art for this book with the subject matter of its contents in mind. I am particularly thankful for the support and patience Jeff has offered me through the string of all-consuming deadlines associated with this book project, and I am also thankful for the enthusiasm with which he took on the project of the cover art. I am proud that his artistic talent can be displayed across the front of this work.

Last, I want to thank, above all, my family for their love, support, and humor, without which I could not accomplish much at all. They are the enduring "dialogue partners" of my life. I am forever indebted to them for teaching me more about the practice of engaged conversation, ethics, and "openness" than I could ever hope to extract from any book.

Introduction: An Invitation to "Play"

"Could you really persuade," he said, "if we don't listen?"
—Plato's *Republic*, 327c

In a wide variety of contexts today, both public and private, we face an outbreak of conflict and division in which there exists a disturbing failure to understand one another in the most vital of matters. Closely partnered with this phenomenon is the widespread rejection of all dialogue in which such an understanding might take place. On the global scene, a dangerous abandonment of dialogical relations and the turn to force abounds between nations, cultures, religions, and tribes. Leaders around the world declare that the time for talk is over and that negotiation is futile. On the national scene, members of differing political parties are unable to have a real conversation with each other about anything. The so-called talking heads on our television sets talk past each other, and sound more like barking dogs than genuine debate partners. On an interpersonal scale, the conversation-stopping phrase "you just can't understand me" because of a difference in gender, race, class, sexual orientation, or ethnicity (take your pick) commonly halts discussion. On occasion, those uninterested in engaging in even the most preliminary verbal exchange utilize the recognizable "talk to the hand" gesture, declaring that all words one might want to speak will fall on deaf ears. This division, spanning such a spectrum of social contexts, is all the more troubling as we recognize the necessity of cultivating more and more fully a global community that can deliberate and act upon shared concerns (concerns such as the health of our environment, human rights, a world economy, depleting natural resources, disease, protecting ourselves from nuclear or biochemical destruction, etc.). In the face of this contemporary demand, we find ourselves confronted with the pressing questions: What causes dialogue to break down? And, what do we do once it has? On the eve of the oft-repeated "time for change," my hope is that we are ready to seek an answer.

This book is an invitation to turn to the philosophical hermeneutics of Hans-Georg Gadamer, which offers a philosophy rich in resources for grappling with questions surrounding communication, understanding, and the varying approaches we might take to others whose ideas are considerably different from our own. While Gadamer's magnum opus *Truth and Method* explicitly concerns itself with discovering how under-

standing works and what makes understanding possible, it simultaneously offers a distinctive philosophy of genuine human engagement in which
true dialogue and understanding can be achieved. It also reveals the
crucial role that such a genuine engagement plays in the sustenance and
nourishment of our human form of life. By focusing on Gadamer's
concept of "play" — the reciprocal and dialogical movement that designates the process of understanding in *Truth and Method* — my aim is to
illuminate the ethical conditions for genuine dialogue and understanding
that emerge from Gadamer's hermeneutic philosophy. I aim also to
highlight the implicit lesson in Gadamer's hermeneutics that preserving
an authentic engagement in "play" with the Other is crucial for our
education, development, and our very existence as human beings. By
bringing to light these aspects of Gadamer's philosophy, I want both to
show that Gadamer's hermeneutic philosophy involves at its core an
ethical philosophy, and to join Gadamer in his effort to better grasp our
productive and destructive modes of human engagement for the purpose
of improving our own practices.

HERMENEUTICS AND ETHICS INTERTWINED

Implicit in Gadamer's philosophical hermeneutics is what I would like to
call, as my title suggests, an "ethics of play." I mean this in three ways.
First, Gadamer's phenomenological analysis of how understanding works
in terms of play reveals to us that there are crucial *ethical conditions* that
must be met for genuine dialogic play to succeed. Second, there is an
implicit *value claim* in Gadamer's work that genuine play with the Other is
ultimately *good* for us as the interactive path of our development as
human beings. Third, Gadamer's theory of understanding as a process of
play is meant *as practical philosophy* (in the style of the older Aristotelian
tradition) to guide our concrete dialogical relations with others so that we
may understand better, and — insofar as understanding is conceived by
Gadamer as our very mode of being and developing in the world — so that
we may come to *live better*.

Those even somewhat familiar with Gadamer's hermeneutics might
wonder why a guide through *Truth and Method* and its ethical dimensions
would focus on "play" rather than concentrate its attention on Gadamer's
famous "fusion of horizons." It is certainly true that the philosophical
world has come to associate Gadamer's notion of understanding with a
"fusion of horizons." Every introduction to Gadamer's philosophy places
a heavy emphasis on this phrase, and Gadamer's most influential critics
tend to focus closely on the notion as well.

Gadamer's notion of understanding as a process of fusion appears to
many of Gadamer's critics (from Betti and Hirsch[1], to Habermas[2], to those
of a Nietzschean-Derridean orientation such as Bernasconi[3] and Caputo[4])

to be fundamentally opposed in various ways to difference, tension, or plurality among viewpoints. It appears to merge ideas in a way that always makes "one" out of two or even *forces* "two" into "one" and, thus, ultimately does violence to otherness, alterity, and resistance. Critics see it as a unifying and homogenizing force that aims to do away with a diversity of perspectives—a process in which one horizon is taken over or assimilated by another more dominant one so that a totalized, univocal, or static end may be reached. These critics see the fusion of horizons to be representative of just what they see to be so *un*ethical about Gadamer's vision of understanding. Once we realize that the fusion of horizons, which Gadamer claims takes place in all understanding, is a fusion between I and Thou, the charge comes through loud and clear. From one side we hear accusations that understanding as "fusion" means submitting to the authority of the Other whose articulation we are trying to understand, taking on the Other's point of view in a way that means giving up our own power of reflection and critique, or even giving up ourselves to the Other. From the other side we hear the concern that fusion amounts to the projection of one's own meaning or interpretation onto that of the Other, which results in the interpreter's ethically suspect denial of the Other's difference, and a failure to recognize the true uniqueness of the Other's point of view that is central to his individuality and personhood.

Though I am as mesmerized as the next reader by Gadamer's image of the fusion of horizons, I worry that the image considered alone is much too susceptible to misinterpretation . . . a misinterpretation which I believe is the cause of much of its criticism. We can avoid a misrepresentation of the process of understanding that constitutes Gadamer's account and practice of hermeneutics if we move beyond our fixation on the fusion of horizons, and expand our focus so that Gadamer's more pervasive concept throughout *Truth and Method*—"play" (*Spiel*)—may come into view. Focusing on Gadamer's notion of understanding as "play" will allow us to see more clearly the way that understanding always remains a dynamic process in which difference is the lifeblood. It will also allow us to retrieve the context in which we can better grasp the meaning of the fusion of horizons.[5]

In referring to play in the context of art alone, much of the secondary literature on Gadamer discusses the concept of play only in its local relevance.[6] Those who sense that its significance might stretch beyond the experience of artworks to, at least, the reading of texts, still find its larger implications to be vague or merely "suggestive," and in need of further explication.[7] I would like to show that "play" has a *global* relevance in philosophical hermeneutics and offer the "further explication" that has been called for. I aim to show that "play" elucidates the very process of understanding *in general*—the understanding which stretches through all our hermeneutic experience, including our encounters with art, with text, with tradition in all its forms, with others in dialogue, and which even constitutes our very mode of being-in-the-world. Grasping Gadamer's notion of understanding as play is the key for appreciating his unique vision of understanding as a dynamic process that requires participants to approach each other with a comportment of "openness" to succeed. This "openness" is characterized by a willingness to truly listen to what the Other has to say and to be transformed by it. Retrieving the concept of play and offering its full development will make it possible to revive the ethical heart of philosophical hermeneutics in the face of Gadamer's most influential critics.

FORM MATTERS

Part I: Gadamer's Hermeneutic Problem

Part I of this book is meant especially for the reader who is new to Gadamer's work. It offers an introduction to his primary questions in *Truth and Method* and his distinct kind of hermeneutics (his *philosophical* hermeneutics). In an effort to abide by one of Gadamer's hermeneutic principles, which states that in order to understand a given text one must understand the question to which it is an answer, part I aims as a whole to elucidate the dubious question mark which has compelled Gadamer to write his magnum opus. This is the question of whether modern science's claim to a monopoly on knowledge is legitimate. The notion that modern scientific method is the *only* means through which "real" truth can be attained is a notion that Gadamer argues dominates the philosophical and popular thinking of his time. Inasmuch as we still find ourselves referring to those sciences that utilize modern scientific method (namely the natural sciences) as the "hard" or "pure" sciences, and consider the social sciences and humanities to be "soft" or inferior sciences, we retain that lasting perception that modern scientific method is the only way to "real" or "certain" knowledge. But this is a perception that is highly questionable to Gadamer, and is in need of confrontation. In order to map out the main problems that trouble Gadamer in *Truth and Method* and outline his main goals in the text, part I of this book gives an account of what Gadamer takes to be modern science's methodological goal of a pure "scientific consciousness," as well as the "aesthetic consciousness" and "historical consciousness" developed by the human sciences of the nineteenth century that mimic it. Here my aim is to explain how, from Gadamer's point of view, all three types of "pure" consciousness fail to account for and achieve the phenomenon of genuine understanding. This first part of the book is meant to offer the contextual background upon which the relevance of Gadamer's concept of play can be understood. It is also meant to invite newcomers to Gadamer's philosophy—especially those who make *interpretation* their main business (whether that is the interpretation of artworks, texts, or historical tradition in general), or those who make *communication* their main business (such as mediators or facilitators)—into the conversation sparked by Gadamer regarding the difficulties associated with the way we "moderns" have come to think about understanding. This part will help the reader to grasp the problems Gadamer sees with this modern view of understanding and to recognize the need for a new, more accurate conception of how understanding really works. Finally, it will prepare the reader for the unique, alternative conception of understanding that Gadamer develops in his *Truth and Method* with his concept of play.

Part II: Gadamer's Concept of Play: Reconceiving the Process of Understanding

Once the need for a new conception of the process of understanding has been explained, part II proceeds to clarify what exactly "play" means for Gadamer. In this part I aim to develop the global significance of "play" in Gadamer's philosophy as the concept that captures the process of *all* understanding. I want to show here that play is the "key" to grasping Gadamer's alternative to the modern scientific notion of knowledge. Because Gadamer's magnum opus is written not in the manner of a logical proof or grand system, but in the form of a developing plot in which the reader comes to acquire, through the discussions of art, history, and language, a better conception of what the process of understanding is, I find that tracing the development of play (as a main character in this plot) is the best way to present the full richness of the concept. This is the purpose of part II, which follows "play's" life through the contexts of art, text, tradition, experience, and dialogue.

There is a special "sense" involved in taking this approach to presentation and examination in the book. Any serious engagement with Gadamer's work leads one to increasingly appreciate the different ways that the form in which content is communicated matters and has an important effect on the listener or reader. Gadamer sends us a message, in both the manner in which he writes and the explicit content he presents, that a human being will not, and cannot, simply change his old conceptions by being handed new ones—or by being handed a set of new premises and conclusions—as if some kind of instantaneous conversion were possible. Instead, learning happens through a slow and thorough process of engagement with new meaning, in which the prejudices with which we begin slowly come to light, and are revised until we reach a transformed sense of things. The logic of Gadamer's own *Truth and Method*, which guides us through such an authentic process of learning by bringing us back to the same themes and insights from multiple perspectives, makes possible a special kind of philosophical experience that could not be had through a more analytic exposition. Inspired by the spirit of such a mode of education, I also aim to create the opportunity for the significance of play to be experienced in its full richness. This is why I have avoided presenting the relevant material in the manner of, say, a succession of Gadamerian principles or punch lines, which would inevitably remain empty without the process, that is, the build up (or more properly the *Bildung*) involved in coming to an enriched understanding of what they mean.

Part III: The Ethical Dimensions of Play

As part II culminates in a discussion of the ultimately dialogic nature of understanding and its play-process, and an acknowledgment that the play we have been considering is a play between "I and Thou,"[8] the reader is now prepared to enter into a discussion of the ethical dimensions of play. Part III endeavors, first, to carefully foreground what I take to be the *ethical conditions* of dialogic play that emerge from Gadamer's discussion. These conditions I call "ethical" for four reasons: (1) they are the necessary "*I-Thou*" relations, or ways that interlocutors must approach each other and treat each other, in order for dialogic play to continue and flourish; (2) these I-Thou relations create an encounter with the Other that is characterized by mutual respect (i.e., treating the Other like a human being who has something meaningful to say, rather than an object to be dominated); (3) these I-Thou relations require a shared commitment and self-disciplined conduct to be achieved; and (4) these I-Thou relations ultimately provide for a process in which mutual human growth can occur, making them I-Thou relations that are directed toward our common human good. The "openness" of interlocutors toward each other that characterizes these I-Thou relations, and distinguishes *genuine* dialogic relations from other more degenerate modes of conversation (what I call modes of "foul play"), is highlighted in this section by comparison to the popular (but problematic) scientific, psychological, and sophistic approaches to the Other.

Part III, second, considers the *value* of play itself. Here I argue that there exists a fully operational (but never explicitly mentioned) value claim in *Truth and Method* that engaging in play is ultimately *good* for us. Play, as the concept emerges in Gadamer's work, reveals itself to be the very activity in which we learn, grow, and flourish as human beings. Recognizing the value of play as the interactive path of human flourishing allows us to better understand how the I-Thou relations necessary for play to succeed are "ethical" (for the fourth reason mentioned), in the sense that they are directed at our human good.

Finally, part III attempts to show the distinctively Aristotelian way in which Gadamer's discussion of play embodies an ethics, or ethical philosophy. The high stakes of Gadamer's discussion of play *as a guide to praxis*, or a practical philosophy, emerges in this section with an exposition of Gadamer's understanding of the intimate connection between theory and practice and the way they endlessly inform each other. This part aims to show how coming to a proper conception of understanding — that is, one that is more phenomenologically correct, or describes more accurately what is really going on when understanding occurs — has an important practical relevance to Gadamer. It aids us past the sorts of obstacles to understanding that we have come to set for ourselves, and guides us in the kinds of dialogical practices in which genuine understanding can emerge.

Part IV: When Ethical Conditions are Lacking

Part IV raises a particular problem that I see with Gadamer's "ethics of play," which brings to light the limits of Gadamer's hermeneutics as a guide to praxis. If Gadamer's hermeneutics is meant to guide us past common obstacles to understanding and to help us engage in better dialogic practices, but at the same time reveals to us that no real dialogue or understanding can even begin without interlocutors sharing a common "openness" toward each other, then it seems as though we are left without direction when we are faced with our biggest hurdle to genuine understanding. This hurdle is the instance in which an "openness" toward (or from) the Other is lacking. It is just where authentic play most problematically breaks down and where we are in desperate need for the most guidance, then, that Gadamer seems unable to help us. His theory provides an explanation for how understanding works and is enriched between those who are already open to each other enough to speak and listen, who already want to understand, and, in a sense, already share a common ethic and basic kind of friendship. But our biggest problem is how we are to cultivate a shared willingness in those people (including ourselves) who *have become "closed"* to the Other. We cannot simply persuade someone through dialogue that understanding is important and that "openness" and a serious acknowledgment of what the Other says is worthwhile, if he has no desire to listen to us. How are we to cultivate the ethical conditions for dialogue in the first place when they appear to be completely lacking?

When faced with a refusal to engage in genuine dialogue, individuals tend to be tempted to either disengage, retreat, and withdraw from any kind of encounter with the Other, or to try to overpower the Other with force. Because Gadamer encourages in us a recognition that our continued to-and-fro engaged "play" with the Other is crucial for our very way of living and flourishing as human beings, we can see that disengagement, the complete restriction of the Other's possibility for participating in play, the elimination of the Other — or any other "game-stopping" moves — are the worst kinds of violence against our human form of life. It is just when we are faced with those who are unwilling to engage in dialogue, then, that we must find new ways of interacting, engaging, *playing* with them. The game must go on.

Gadamer inspires in us a recognition of our general ethical responsibility to engage in an ongoing play-process with the Other, and to strive for the genuine understanding that can emerge from it. We are left, then, feeling also a responsibility to try to cultivate the conditions for such an engagement when they are lacking. But how? Though Gadamer may not have offered us an answer, he has certainly led us to this new question of increasing contemporary relevance. It is up to us to carry on the conversation begun by him in relation to our current problems and pressing demands. Might we find a way to appropriate the conceptual resources available in Gadamer's rich notion of play to help us carve out a space of human engagement that fosters a first opening or reopening to dialogue? Might we broaden Gadamer's "ethics of play" to guide us in scenarios where genuine dialogue has disintegrated? Might we use Gadamer to move beyond Gadamer? Surely, it is worth the effort to make a first attempt.

NOTES

1. See Emilio Betti's "Hermeneutics as the General Methodology of the *Geisteswissenschaften*," in *Contemporary Hermeneutics*, ed. Josef Bleicher (London and New York: Routledge & Kegan Paul, 1980), and E. D. Hirsch's *Validity in Interpretation* (New Haven and London: Yale University Press, 1967). These early critics of Gadamer voice the similar worry that the "fusion of horizons" that occurs in understanding, as Gadamer sees it, inevitably comes down to our own projection of meaning onto that of the Other, the past meaning of the text, or tradition. In this case our interpretation becomes too subjective.

2. See Jürgen Habermas's "Review of *Truth and Method* " in *The Hermeneutic Tradition*, ed. Gayle L. Ormiston and Alan D. Schrift (Albany: SUNY Press, 1990). Habermas's worry about understanding as a fusion of horizons is that it involves our submission to the meaning of the Other or past tradition, and allows the oppressive power of tradition to be perpetuated without resistance and critique.

3. See Robert Bernasconi's "'You Don't Know What I'm Talking About': Alterity and the Hermeneutic Ideal," in *The Specter of Relativism: Truth, Dialogue, and* Phronesis *in Philosophical Hermeneutics*, ed. Lawrence Schmidt (Evanston, IL: Northwestern University Press, 1995). Bernasconi's claim is that understanding for Gadamer is a force that always attempts to assimilate otherness, difference, or alterity, in the quest for the "agreement" inherent in a fusion of horizons.

4. See John Caputo's *Radical Hermeneutics* (Bloomington and Indianapolis: Indiana University Press, 1987), where he claims that Gadamer's hermeneutics attempts to smooth over (and thus ignore) all the ruptures, gaps, and breaks in experience in pursuit of "metaphysical comfort." It tries to resolve all questions and discontinuities, rather than face the difficulties of recognizing those that cannot be answered or reconciled into some harmonious whole.

5. By turning toward the concept of "play," my intention is not to ignore the concept of the "fusion of horizons" or sever its connection with Gadamer's notion of understanding (and thereby sidestep the criticisms of Gadamer that are tied up with that concept). Rather, I wish to put the fusion of horizons back into its proper context as

one of the concepts through which Gadamer tries to articulate his unique vision of understanding—*one* concept that can be grasped more properly when understood itself in terms of the dynamic movement of "play," which I argue pervades the whole of *Truth and Method*. When the fusion of horizons is understood in terms of a dynamic process between different individual players, many common criticisms lose their ground.

6. For instance, one of the most influential introductions to hermeneutics—Richard Palmer's *Hermeneutics: Interpretation Theory in Schleiermacher, Dilthey, Heidegger, and Gadamer* (Evanston, Ill.: Northwestern University Press, 1969)—which has been credited for bringing Gadamer to the consciousness of the English-speaking world, discusses the notion of play or game only in the context of art and Gadamer's critique of aesthetic consciousness (171–76). This is really the model for most commentaries on the concept. To be fair, Palmer does, in one sentence, allude to play's larger significance when he suggests that with the notion of the game, "Gadamer has found a model . . . which can serve as a basis for substantiating the dialectical and ontological character of his own hermeneutics" (174). How exactly this is the case still needs to be developed.

7. This is, for example, how Georgia Warnke characterizes play in her book *Gadamer: Hermeneutics, Tradition and Reason* (Stanford: Stanford University Press, 1987), 48.

8. The language of "I and Thou," which represents the relationship between two human beings as opposed to the relationship between subject and object (i.e., "I and It"), was made famous by Martin Buber in his text *I and Thou*, trans. Walter Kaufmann (New York: Touchstone, 1970). Though Gadamer's own sense of this intersubjective relationship in which understanding emerges is different in important ways from Buber's, he repeatedly uses the phrase as a way of making clear that understanding is an event that always occurs between human beings in language, or between interlocutors. I aim to highlight how this always entails an important ethical component.

Part I

Gadamer's Hermeneutic Problem

Chapter 1

Facing the Inadequate Model of Modern Science

THE HERMENEUTIC PROBLEM

In its most basic terms, hermeneutics can be defined as the theory and practice of interpretation. In his magnum opus *Truth and Method* (*Wahrheit und Methode*), Hans-Georg Gadamer is concerned with the problem of hermeneutics, or the "phenomenon of understanding and of the correct interpretation of what has been understood."[1] Gadamer insists that the phenomenon of understanding (*Verstehen*) reaches far beyond the limits of the conception of "knowledge" put forth by modern science, whose standards of truth and the proper method for coming to know such truth have come to dominate philosophical and popular thinking. He believes that, surely, there is a kind of understanding that can be achieved aside from following the methodological procedures of modern science. Though Gadamer never offers a strict definition of modern scientific method, we can see from his writings that he has in mind an inductive method that is ruled by a cycle of observation, hypothesis, experimentation, and verification. It is a method that must be repeatable by anyone and is supposed to provide a prejudice-less examination of facts. The ultimate goal of this method is to discover the regularities or natural laws inherent in the world, in order to predict future phenomena and gain some sort of mastery over them.[2] Gadamer argues that the so-called scientific knowledge (*wissenschaftliche Erkenntnis*) that is produced by this method cannot exhaust the domain of genuine knowing and that *truth* cannot be limited to a set of natural laws. Science (*Wissenschaft*) itself, Gadamer argues, should not be narrowed to the specific methodological work of the natural sciences (*Naturwissenschaften*), as has been done in the modern era,[3] for this ignores the unique, genuine modes of knowing involved in the work of the human sciences (*Geisteswissenschaften*).[4] Gadamer argues that the modern restrictions on what constitutes genuine knowledge and truth run contrary to the nonmethodological or "extra-scientific" experiences we have in which we surely come to understand something we did not understand before, and undergo some kind of enriching transformation, development, or education in the process. Gadamer maintains that the process of understanding is something that occurs, for instance, in the experience of a work of art, in the reading and interpreting of a text, in the engagement with tradition in all its forms, and in our conversations with others. We cannot ignore, Gadamer urges, that in all of these encounters "insights are acquired and truths are known" (TM, xxi) that cannot be attained through the means of scientific method. No "scientific" investigation of a stage-play, a painting, a song, a novel, an argument, and so forth, can replace what is learned in our basic experiences of watching, listening, or reading in which we become caught up in what is communicated to us; no examination of "facts" can enable us to grasp the *meaning* that speaks to us through them, which reveals that modern scientific method is, at the very least, a limited means of acquiring knowledge.

In an even bolder claim, which radically calls into question modern science's notion of knowledge and spotlights its limitations, Gadamer asserts that the phenomenon of understanding is something that "pervades all human relations to the world" (TM, xxii)—relations that precede any deliberate methodical acts on the part of the subject or scientist. He reminds us that Heidegger has "shown convincingly that understanding is not just one of the various possible behaviors of the subject but the mode of being of Dasein itself" (TM, xxx). Hermeneutics, Gadamer tells us, is used in his work to denote "the basic being-in-motion of Dasein that constitutes its finitude and historicity, and hence embraces the whole of his experience of the world" (TM, xxx). This is Gadamer's first sign to us that his hermeneutic project is an ontological one. Unlike the older tradition of (theological and philological) hermeneutics, which was concerned with the understanding and correct interpretation of written texts, Gadamer's hermeneutics has to do with the way we exist as human beings. Since understanding is seen here to be not just a phenomenon that occurs when reading a text, but our *primordial way of being in the world*, the scope of the hermeneutic problem, as Gadamer sees it, stretches throughout the entirety of our human experience. For him, "the province of hermeneutics is universal" (TM, xxxiv). The hermeneutic problem is one, for Gadamer, that touches every corner of human life and is, thus, a problem having to do with the very *being* of the human being, who is in fact an *understanding* being and an *interpreting* being.

It is important to point out, then, that the hermeneutic "problem" of which Gadamer speaks is quite different from the problem of the older tradition of hermeneutics, whose task—as a technical art of interpretation—was to develop special methodological rules for interpreting difficult religious or literary texts. Since understanding designates our very way of being in the world to Gadamer, he sees it as a primary activity that precedes any deliberate, methodical pursuits. He wants not to come up with rules for us to follow in order to understand, but to discover through a phenomenological analysis (or descriptive study) what understanding itself really is and how it really works.

Gadamer recognizes that, if the "truth" that he claims is "known" in our extra-scientific experiences is going to be philosophically legitimated as real, genuine truth, then what is required of him is a deeper investigation into the phenomenon of understanding itself. Because the narrow, modern scientific conception of "knowledge" does not account for the broader scale of experiences in which we undergo the transformation of coming-to-an-understanding, and so misconceives the true phenomena of understanding itself, Gadamer sees that we are in need of new and more accurate notions of knowledge and truth (*Begriffs der Erkenntnis und der Wahrheit*). In an effort to develop these better notions, Gadamer's purpose becomes "to discover what is common to all modes of understanding" (TM, xxxi). He, thus, asks the philosophical question—not just of modern science and its modes of experience, nor only of the so-called human sciences, *but of all human experience of the world and human living*—"how is understanding possible?" (TM, xxx). It is this guiding question that causes Gadamer to inquire into the phenomenon of understanding itself and see how it is that hermeneutic experience happens at all. This makes Gadamer's hermeneutic problem a *philosophical* problem, and his unique brand of hermeneutics *philosophical* hermeneutics.

TURN TO THE HUMAN SCIENCES

To help Gadamer discover what makes the process of understanding in general possible—beyond (and prior to) the limits of scientific knowledge—he sets out to find and examine those experiences of truth that occur outside the confines of modern scientific method. He, thus, turns to the human sciences (*Geisteswissenschaften*) and the experiences of art, history, and philosophy.

In the human sciences, Gadamer observes that historical tradition (*geschichtliche Überlieferung*) in all its forms—the forms of art, text, law, religion, philosophy, and any other "spiritual creations of the past" (TM, 65, 165)—is made the object of investigation. Tradition is *what* is investigated in the human sciences, but it is investigated in a way, as Gadamer hopes to show, that is quite different from the way in which objects are approached and examined in the natural sciences. First of all, a piece of tradition—a drama, a painting, a text, a law, a legend, a philosophy, a religion, and so on—is not, strictly speaking, an "object" at all. It is, rather, a "creation of spirit" or an articulation by some human being—some "Thou"—who speaks to us from the past and presents to us something meaningful about our reality for us to understand and recognize *as true*. In tradition, Gadamer argues, a meaningful "claim to truth" (*Wahrheitan-spruch*) about our common world is made for us to hear and grasp, so that in tradition "*truth comes to speech*" (TM, xxiii). This means that in the human sciences, as Gadamer puts it, understanding already belongs to what we are trying to understand. An investigation of a piece of tradition, then, does not consist simply in collecting and examining its "facts" in the manner of the natural scientist. It consists, rather, in listening to the articulation or statement about our world that is being communicated to us, and in trying to grasp its meaning. Gadamer argues: "Fundamentally, the experience of historical tradition reaches far beyond those aspects of it that can be objectively investigated. It is true or untrue not only in the sense concerning which historical criticism decides, but always mediates truth in which one must *try to share*" (TM, xxiii). Gadamer seems to be telling us here that if we treat the voice of tradition that speaks to us across time simply as the kind of "object" studied by natural science—a mute piece of matter, or strictly formal "thing," devoid of any meaningful content—we will close our ears to the claim resounding from it and miss the meaning that it presents for us to grasp.[5] We will improve our chances of hearing and grasping the claim to truth that is made if we do not *objectify* tradition, but approach it as another subject who understands something and has something to say to us. Tradition is a *speaker, mediator, communicator* of truth with which we must engage, as Gadamer will show, in a kind of *dialogue* in order to understand the significance of what is being articulated.

This point illuminates a second related way in which the investigation of tradition, in which the human sciences are engaged, differs from investigation in the natural sciences. Whereas the natural scientist is commanded to *distance* herself from her object of investigation as much as possible, in order to properly observe from a neutral standpoint its formal attributes alone; the human scientist must *engage* the voice of the Other that speaks through tradition in order to understand the meaning of what is said. The natural scientist attempts, as modern method prescribes, to remove herself as much as possible from her investigation. She tries to disregard everything she already knows, all her old opinions, attitudes, prejudices, expectations, interests, desires—that is, the whole context of meaning that she carries with her. She does this so that her "objects" can be seen clearly and purely "in-themselves," untainted by any "subjective" projections. It is only through these procedures of abstraction, it is believed, that "objectivity" (a standpoint devoid of personal perspective or interpretation) can be achieved. But, in trying to understand the meaning of what is articulated in tradition—a meaning that Gadamer argues can only "live again" if it is received and recognized by us as significant in the context of our world—we cannot try to remove ourselves and our context from the process of communication in which we are trying to participate. Distancing ourselves from tradition in the style of the natural scientist would ultimately mean avoiding the kind of encounter with tradition in which we might come to understand the truth spoken through it. Following the special procedures of scientific method, then, will not help us to acquire the kind of understanding that occurs only in the *communication of something meaningful* between human beings. It will instead hinder the engagement necessary for such communication to take place.

Finally, there is a third important difference that Gadamer emphasizes between the natural sciences and the human sciences. This last key difference pertains to the divergent goals and objectives of the two sciences. Gadamer repeatedly suggests that the goal of domination is built right into the objectifying method of the natural sciences, where making what one studies into an "object" is itself an attempt to become active "master" over and against a passive "thing." This is the first step in a process of breaking down the thing studied into its parts so that it may be more easily controlled and manipulated. But, Gadamer proclaims, whereas the natural sciences' goal is to understand the workings of the natural world in order to *predict* and *control* future phenomena, the human sciences' ultimate aim is to *share* in the meaning that tradition hands down. The human sciences, thus, do not endeavor to dominate what they study, but rather to *participate* with it (as we've mentioned) in a kind of communication.

We might better recognize the key differences mentioned between the natural and human sciences if we imagine a scenario where both natural and human scientists are studying side by side at the same research site. Let's imagine both kinds of scientist at the famous caves in Lascaux, France, when they were first discovered. One natural scientist is there, perhaps, to collect evidence that he can use to test the age of the cave and its structural integrity. Perhaps he is trying to determine whether the cave is safe enough for more researchers, students, or tourists to enter. Another natural scientist is there to regularly test the dye used in the cave paintings to determine if it is deteriorating or being compromised by exposure to carbon dioxide. A human scientist, an anthropologist, is there to investigate what the cave was originally used for. This human scientist is interested in what the cave meant to the people who used it. Was it a holy place? Were rites of passage carried out there? Another human scientist is there to study the paintings themselves as works of art and consider what the horses and bulls represent. Are these creatures depicted as gods? Are the animals presented as threatening, or as beasts that have lovingly sacrificed their lives for the hungry? The main difference we see between the activities of the natural and human scientists in this imagined scenario is that while the natural scientists go to work gathering an infinite number of "objective" facts in order to determine what we can do with the caves, only the human scientists try to grasp the meaning of the caves and consider their real significance.

Whereas the modern scientific model of knowledge is marked by the subject's *distance* from and *control* over his object, the kind of understanding that occurs in the human sciences is characterized by the *participation* of I and Thou in a communication which results in the *sharing* of a common meaning. In looking to the human sciences for an account of the distinctive kind of work in which they are engaged, Gadamer finds that the human sciences of the nineteenth century had come to understand themselves on the model of natural science and had, thus, adopted its conceptions of knowledge and truth, as well as its method. Any understanding of the human sciences' *unique* mode of knowing, which Gadamer had hoped to find, had been pushed to the background of their view.[6] Natural science had become the yardstick against which *all* science was measured, and its method had become considered the *only* way to produce certain, reliable knowledge. It was only by the utilization of the natural science's mode of investigation that the human sciences of the nineteenth century could maintain their status as "sciences" at all. So, taking up the assumption that truth is "out there" in the objects of the world and can be discovered or known in the mind of the unprejudiced investigator, human scientists, too, set out to obtain that supposed prejudice-less depiction of the facts hailed as "objective knowledge"—the *only* kind of knowledge.

Gadamer sees this occur in the fields of aesthetics and history in the nineteenth century, where special abstraction procedures of "aesthetic consciousness" (*ästhetische Bewußtsein*) and "historical consciousness" (*historische Bewußtsein*) were developed to mimic the pure "scientific consciousness" (*wissenschaftliche Bewußtsein*) of the natural sciences. With these procedures, the human sciences believed they could achieve the same objective knowledge of aesthetic and historical objects that the natural sciences had achieved of natural objects. Gadamer, however, shows us how these procedures resulted, in the end, in a failure to reach understanding.

Aesthetics in the Era of Erlebniskunst

Gadamer observes that in modern aesthetics the task of grasping a work of art is taken to be achievable only through "aesthetic consciousness," which depends upon a process of abstraction that Gadamer calls "aesthetic differentiation" (TM, 85) (*ästhetische Unterscheidung*).[7] This consists in directing one's attention toward only the "aesthetic" or "formal" elements of the work, and disregarding all "extra-aesthetic" elements such as purpose, function, content, context, and concept in order to make it visible as a "pure" work of art that exists in its own right. The work of art is conceived, here, as consisting of its aesthetic elements alone. If we are to grasp it in its purity, then, we must see it with purely aesthetic eyes. This means freeing it of any ties to the world that would cause us to take up a moral, religious, or intellectual stance toward it. These sorts of "nonaesthetic" stances toward the work are, here, regarded as a projection of values and biases that would infect and taint our experience of the work and keep us from seeing it in its aesthetic purity and autonomy. To view an icon of the Virgin Mary with aesthetic consciousness, then, one would need to concentrate only on the color, line, and shape of her figure and to disregard any religious connotation connected to the image. In order to produce, in the modern era, a proper "aesthetic experience" (*ästhetische Erlebnis*), one must carry out the twofold procedure of (1) isolating the work in its formal elements alone and removing it from the world of which it is thought to be essentially independent, and (2) removing ourselves from our own context of meaning, which is thought to pollute our vision of the work proper.

This peculiar notion of what it means to have a proper encounter with a work of art makes a bit more sense when we consider more closely the conception of art as "*Erlebniskunst*" to which it corresponds. In the modern era, Gadamer explains, art (*Kunst*) itself is understood as something that is based on experience (*Erlebnis*). Art is defined as the creation of an inspired genius out of a miraculous, unconscious, free expression of his lived experience, or what is called the "flash of genius." The word *Erlebnis* means both (1) the immediate, first-person, lived feeling that precedes interpretation or communication (a kind of material to be shaped) and (2) the lasting significance that results from this "flow" of feeling, which we are likely to call "*an* experience" (TM, 61). In Wilhelm Dilthey's work, which attempts to give a philosophical grounding to the objectivity of the human sciences, the concept *Erlebnis* designates what is directly and immediately *given* to consciousness[8] and the ultimate material for all imaginative creation. For Dilthey, life (*Leben*) objectifies itself into structures of meaning—into experiences (*Erlebnisse*). An experience (like an adventure) is a rounded out whole that stands out against or interrupts the regular flow of one's life, but also relates back to the whole of the individual life in which it occurs—for it is this relation between the experience and the individual life that constitutes the experience's significance or meaning.[9] An experience, in the era of *Erlebniskunst*, is thought to reach its ultimate expression in the work of art, in particular, the work of the artistic genius.

The work that the genius produces out of his personal experience is seen, in modern aesthetics, to be a "free" creation, in that its significance is supposed to be inherent or internal to the work itself, and not tied to or dependent on any broader context or tradition in which the artist might happen to find himself. It is a "free" creation because it is significant in itself. It must, then, be judged on its own terms (that is, on its internal aesthetic structure and the feeling of pleasure that the structure incites in us[10]), not by nonaesthetic (such as moral or intellectual) standards.

From the standpoint that true art is "free" art, all creations that *do* depend on something traditional for their significance to be grasped (such as the general knowledge of a religious or secular story) end up being demoted to the level of "lower" art or even "non-art." For example, allegory during this time was denied the status of genuine art, because it remained tied to concepts outside itself, which it pointed to and depended upon for its meaning—a "tie" or relationship established by (traditional) convention. It could not, thus, be the independent product of unconscious genius alone. Symbol on the other hand, which was thought to be inherently significant (i.e., having an inward unity of appearance and meaning which was established metaphysically and could not be ex-hausted by some concept), was expanded to a universal aesthetic princi-ple. Art proper was seen to be the product of the free symbol-making activity of the mind. As Gadamer explains, modern aesthetics "sought to emphasize precisely the unity of appearance and meaning in the symbolic in order thereby to justify aesthetic autonomy against the claims of the concept" (TM, 79). Art (*Kunst*), as the "free" expression of the genius's experience (*Erlebnis*), itself became defined as *Erlebniskunst,* which could only be grasped in its pure aesthetic form through another experience—a free and immediate "aesthetic experience" that depended upon the abstraction procedures of aesthetic consciousness.

We can see how this modern conception of art as free, independent, and significant in its aesthetic or formal elements alone corresponds with the idea that a proper aesthetic experience involves the effort to abstract context, concept, and content (or everything that is considered "non-art") from one's encounter with it. But Gadamer illuminates how this pair of concepts—art-based-on-experience (*Erlebniskunst*) and aesthetic con-sciousness (*ästhetische Bewußtsein*)—forms a picture of aesthetics that is wrought with problematic consequences.

The biggest problem for Gadamer is that the effort of modern aesthet-ics to conceive of art as the unconscious creation of genius, unrelated to and untouchable by the judgments of the old authorities of reason, tradition, and morality, has led art to be defined inevitably as beautiful "appearance" in *opposition* to reality.[11] Now, according to Gadamer, art may have acquired its "freedom" and attained its autonomy in some aesthetic domain where the laws of beauty alone rule; but this freedom and separation from our world means that art has become relegated to the realm of "mere" appearance and associated with illusion, dream, and veil—*not* reality and *not* truth that is to be known. Aesthetic experience, consequently, has taken on the character of "an adventure producing a temporary intoxication from which one reawakens to one's true being" (TM, 133). The experience of art has come to be understood as disjointed from our experience of the rest of the world. It is conceived as an escape, a source of aesthetic pleasure or entertainment, but unable to teach us anything about the world in which we live.

Art in the modern era, Gadamer argues, has been emptied out of its truth. Simultaneously, aesthetic experience has lost its status as a mode of knowing, and this is just Gadamer's frustration. Through the nineteenth century conceptions of art-based-on-experience (*Erlebniskunst*) and aesthetic consciousness (*ästhetische Bewußtsein*), we have inherited a notion of aesthetic experience that does not do justice to our true experience of art. Gadamer maintains that when we *truly* encounter art, we do not simply enter into an adventurous dream world or feel some kind of pleasure. Rather, we become connected to our shared world in a new and profound way. A real work of art tries to say something about the world in which we live. It tries to point out some aspect of our reality, show it to us in a particular way, and in doing so make a meaningful claim about our world. When we experience art we, in turn, try to grasp what the work is trying to articulate and *understand its meaning*. We do not walk away from the encounter feeling as if we have *simply* enjoyed ourselves, but knowing that we have learned something more about our world and that we have undergone some enriching transformation in the process. As an example of this we might consider, for instance, our experience of a novel or film that makes us realize the trivial nature of our daily worries and the overwhelmingly brief moment of our human life. In this sort of encounter, art has a kind of force on us that makes us reach a more profound understanding of our human condition. It may even make us change our old habits and transform our lives. Here art does much more than make us "feel" something. It educates us about our world and our existence in it.

Gadamer insists that it is a mistake to view art as disconnected from reality or as some otherworldly realm of appearance. First of all, the artist does not himself live, experience, or create in a vacuum, but always does so within an influential historical context—a context in which his work will inevitably find its significance. Second, art is not merely an unknowing, unconscious upsurge of expression, but an articulation *of something*— some truth about our shared world—that is meant to be *recognized* by us. Gadamer states that the aesthetic myth of the free invention of genius is

> an exaggeration that does not stand up to reality . . . the choice of material and the forming of it . . . do not proceed from the free discretion of the artist and are not the mere expression of his inner life. Rather, the artist addresses people whose minds are prepared and chooses what promises to have an effect on them. He himself stands in the same tradition as the public he is addressing and which he gathers around him. . . . The player, sculptor, or viewer is never simply swept away into a strange world of magic, of intoxication, of dream; rather, it is always his own world, and he comes to belong to it more fully by recognizing himself more profoundly in it. There remains a continuity of meaning which links the work of art with the existing world. (TM, 133–34)

Against the notion that art is produced out of the immediacy of experiences (*Erlebnisse*) from an independent, unconscious, flash of inspiration, waiting to be grasped by another independent, immediate, aesthetic experience, Gadamer declares: "The pantheon of art is not a timeless present that presents itself to a pure aesthetic consciousness, but the act of mind and spirit that has collected and gathered itself historically . . . art is knowledge and experiencing an artwork means sharing in that knowledge" (TM, 97). For Gadamer, the methodological conception of aesthetic experience (*Erlebnis*), which seems to always reduce experience to a feeling of pleasure, fails to account for and achieve the genuine understanding that occurs when we truly experience art. He believes that it is the phenomenological return to aesthetic experience (*Erfahrung*), which captures the way in which experience is an "undergoing" of genuine reality and truth, that will help do justice to the unique mode of knowing that is involved in the encounter with a work of art.

Historical Research in the Era of the "Historical School"

Just as Gadamer saw an effort in the procedures of "aesthetic consciousness" to abstract oneself—that is, one's attitudes, values, presuppositions, and context of meaning—from one's encounter with the work of art in order to see it "in itself," he sees again a similar attempt at self-forgetfulness (*Selbstvergessenheit*) in the procedures of "historical consciousness" (*historische Bewußtsein*), which aim to grasp the history of mankind as a whole on its own terms. Gadamer explains that the historical school (of which Leopold von Ranke and Johann Gustav Droysen are representatives) wanted to understand the continuity of universal history, not based on any criterion that lies outside of history, but *on its own* from historical tradition itself. The historical school arose in reaction against Hegel's teleological vision of history that viewed historical world spirit as ultimately progressing toward its completion or end (*telos*) in which final self-knowledge would be achieved. The historical school conceived of history as a "growing sum," in which historical events emerge in successive order, each conditioning the next and linking together to form a cohesive unity. But for the historical school "there exists neither an end of history nor anything outside it" (TM, 199). The historical school believed that history has a unity and meaning *in itself* that can be grasped, not by speculative philosophy, but only by the historical research done by an historical being. A universal historical worldview (*historische Weltanschauung*)—a view of the whole of history—can be achieved according to the historical school, but only if one does away with all preconceived notions that find, or want to find, the perfection of history either at its beginning in classical antiquity, or at the highpoint of the Enlightenment. Any such notions of progress and regress involve positing some criterion that is beyond history. For the historical school, what is distinctive about history is the rich variety of individual phenomena, which constitutes its value and meaning (TM, 202). If the historian is going to really see history as it truly is, he must eliminate prior notions of perfection from his view and achieve an impartiality that allows him to see each historical event or era as having its own significance in itself. Gadamer explains: "To think historically now means to acknowledge that each period has its own right to exist, its own perfection" (TM, 201). To achieve historical impartiality (*historische Gerechtigkeit*) one must, as Ranke expressed it, "extinguish oneself" (*sich auslöschen*) or free oneself of one's prejudices, principles, and concepts in order to see each historical phenomenon as equally valuable, as if from a God's eye view. This self-forgetting is what constituted, for the historical school, "historical consciousness." Gadamer, though, sees it as an attempt to transcend one's finite view in order to achieve the infinite understanding of God. To defend this reading, Gadamer quotes Ranke as saying: "I imagine the Deity—if I may allow myself this observation—as seeing the whole of historical humanity in its totality (since no time lies before the Deity), and finding it all equally valuable" (TM, 210). Gadamer interprets Ranke as saying that the more the historian is "able to recognize the unique, indestructible value of every phenomenon—that is, to think historically— the more his thought is God-like" (TM, 210).

This historical consciousness was transformed into an epistemology for the human sciences by Dilthey, who Gadamer calls the interpreter of the historical worldview described above. Dilthey took it as his task to answer the question of how historical knowledge is possible, and to give knowledge of the historical world philosophical grounding, as Kant had done before him with regard to knowledge of the natural world. He wanted to complement Kant's *Critique of Pure Reason* with his own *Critique of Historical Reason*. Dilthey argued that what is ultimately "given" to consciousness in the human sciences are structures of meaning. These structures of meaning find their center in the individual, out of which they build themselves into larger and larger units. The smallest unit, as Dilthey understood it, is the individual's "experience" (*Erlebnis*, of which we spoke earlier), while the largest unit is universal history itself—a grand expression of our individual lived experiences (*Erlebnisse*). For Dilthey, "the structures of meaning we meet in the human sciences," such as in artworks and historical texts, can be understood and interpreted by tracing them back to the ultimate/basic units "given" to consciousness— those units of the individual's lived experience (*Erlebnis*) from which they emerged. Through historical consciousness one can grasp *the whole of history* and achieve "objective knowledge" of it. This was for Dilthey (much like Ranke's God-like view) a state of "universal sympathy" where one can transcend the prejudices and preferences of one's own time and see the value of all eras (even simultaneously).

Although the representatives of the historical school wanted to understand history without the use of any preconceived "idea" or presupposi-
tion, Gadamer is eager to point out that they themselves began with their
own prejudice. The prejudice was that history forms some kind of unity
that can be understood as a whole. Gadamer argues that the idea of a
"unified" history, and the notion of the "continuity" or "coherence" of
events that constitute this unity, "is primarily formal in nature and does
not imply any actual contents. It too is like an a priori of research that
invites one to penetrate ever more deeply into the complexities of
historical continuity" (TM, 208). Historical consciousness, which is meant
to see history on its own terms "by itself" or even "in-itself" without the
use of any presuppositions, actually depends upon a prejudice which
directs its work. It not only assumes that history is a unified thing, it also
assumes that it is possible, somehow, to understand *as a whole* something
of which we are always inside. Both presuppositions Gadamer strongly
contests. Gadamer argues that (1) as long as history is an ongoing process,
it cannot be grasped as a complete totality, but furthermore, (2) because
we (and our understanding) always exist inside of history, we can never
be in a position to see history as a whole in the "objective" way that the
historical school had in mind. The sort of objectivity that the historical
school imagined would require us to be able to step outside of the history
in which we always exist. Gadamer insists that the infinite understanding
of world history that the historical school tried to achieve is not possible
for finite beings as ourselves.

By disregarding such facts of our human situation, Gadamer finds that
"historical consciousness was supposed to rise above its own relativity in
a way that made objectivity in the human sciences possible" (TM, 234). He
urges us to see, thus, that historical consciousness attempts to follow the
methodological procedures of the natural sciences and aims to operate on
their model. He states:

> The essence of the experimental method consists in rising above the subjec-
> tive fortuitousness of observation and with the help of method attaining
> knowledge of natural laws. Similarly, the human sciences endeavor to rise
> methodologically above the subjective fortuitousness of their own standpoint
> in history through the tradition accessible to them, and thus attain objective
> historical knowledge. (TM, 236)

This affinity with the natural sciences was the very thing, Gadamer
argues, that Dilthey wanted to prove in order to win for the historical and
human studies the status of "genuine" science. But, Gadamer insists, the
methodological abstraction which is involved in historical consciousness—the "self-forgetting"—fails to account for the real experience (*Erfahrung*) in which we come to understand historical tradition. Grasping the
meaning of tradition involves relating that meaning to our current world,
which we cannot do if we try to forget ourselves and the context in which

we live. Furthermore, conceiving of history as ultimately the *expressions* of individual life-experiences (*Erlebnisse*) that are to be deciphered or re-experienced by us if they are to be understood, does not do justice to the real *knowledge* that is gained in studying history. This knowledge is not a kind of biographical knowledge of other people's private experiences, but a knowledge of the truths of our shared world to which we are all bound.

In short, the ideal of "historical consciousness," according to Gadamer, has followed the model of modern scientific method. It has conceived of historical tradition as a "thing in itself" to be grasped only through a kind of self-forgetting, rather than something of which we are always a part and whose meaning can be grasped only when we relate it to our own lives. Because of this, Gadamer argues, historical consciousness fails to account for and achieve the understanding of tradition that truly takes place in the historical sciences.

BEYOND THE QUARREL BETWEEN THE SCIENCES

We have seen that the modern scientific method of the natural sciences, which the procedures of aesthetic and historical consciousness mimic, is a method characterized largely by the subject's objectification of what he wants to know, and his attempt to achieve objectivity by removing all interests, values, expectations, and interpretations from his investigation. Gadamer has shown us that this method is, *to begin with*, an altogether inappropriate method for study in the human sciences due to the different kinds of objects the human sciences investigate (namely "creations of spirit" that *say* and *mean* something) and the different purpose of investigation in the human sciences (namely, to grasp that meaning). Gadamer has shown us that although modern science claims to have a monopoly on knowledge, its methodology is quite limited, since it is unable to bring about an *understanding of meaning*. If we restrict knowledge to what can be achieved by the procedures of natural science alone, we ignore the unique kind of knowledge that occurs in the human sciences. For Gadamer, this is clearly an inappropriate restriction.

But, it is important to recognize that Gadamer is not *simply* trying to distinguish between the natural and human sciences based on differences in their objects and purposes of investigation. He is not just trying to claim that the natural sciences have an appropriate conception of "truth," "knowledge," and "method" when it comes to the study of natural objects, but that these conceptions cannot be stretched to accommodate the—equally genuine, but wholly different—kind of truth and knowledge appropriate to the human sciences. Gadamer's criticism of modern science's conception of understanding cuts much deeper than this. Gadamer insists that, in looking to the human sciences, he is not trying to "revive the ancient dispute on method between the natural and human sciences," but to "bring into consciousness something which that methodological dispute serves only to conceal and neglect, something that does not so much confine or limit modern science as precede it and make it possible" (TM, xxix). What is interesting to Gadamer about the human sciences is that they reveal to us a mode of knowing distinct from that of modern scientific research, which is quite close to, and teaches us something about, the very basic (premethodical) kind of understanding that permeates our experience of the world at large. The kind of knowing that arises in the appropriation of tradition, which is the work of the human sciences, is not something we just acquire as a part of academic study; it is a crucial part of our everyday form of life. To discover how understanding works in the human sciences is to discover a clue as to how understanding on its most basic and general level works. Gadamer states: "The hermeneutics developed here is not, therefore, a methodology of the human sciences, but an attempt to understand what the human sciences truly are, beyond their methodological self-consciousness, and what connects them with the totality of our experience of the world" (TM, xxiii). Gadamer aims to show us that there is a very basic kind of understanding that precedes and makes possible the kind of methodical knowledge we find in science, which science, nonetheless, does not recognize. In wanting to know what makes understanding *in general* possible (in all modes of human experience from its most basic, spontaneous appearance to its most methodical and scientific manifestation), Gadamer will have to battle—in a way that cuts much deeper than any quarrel between the sciences ever could—our deeply ingrained notions of truth, knowledge, subject, object, experience, method, and objectivity.

Through Gadamer's critique of aesthetic and historical consciousness, Gadamer not only endeavors to show us that the modern scientific method (which is the model upon which aesthetic and historical consciousness are built) is a wholly inappropriate means for coming to understand the meaning that speaks to us through the artwork and other forms of tradition. Rather, he also endeavors to show us that there is something fundamentally wrong with the ideal of modern scientific methodology itself—that is, its peculiar ideal of "objectivity."[12] There is something deeply *delusional* about modern science's notion that the scientist can accomplish the task of completely removing herself and her prejudices from her investigation, and there is something truly misconceived about modern science's notion of a noninterpretive kind of experience. Modern science deludes itself about the character of knowledge itself if it thinks that it could be a "pure-seeing" in the sense of a view of things from outside of ourselves—for this is simply not a human possibility.

This assessment finds its first expression in Gadamer's critique of aesthetic consciousness, which aims at a "pure seeing" of the work of art "in-itself" or in its purely aesthetic form. Gadamer argues that this goal is itself rooted in a misunderstanding of how perception and experience works and is entrenched in what he calls an "epistemological dogmatism." Gadamer argues, first of all, that "our perception is never a simple reflection of what is given to the senses" (TM, 90) but, rather, always a "seeing-as." By this he means that it is not the case that atoms or units of data are given to the senses somehow independent of what they are related to, so that we might perceive what is before us, for instance, as a bright, red, round, smooth phenomenon (i.e., purely aesthetically). On the contrary, we perceive the phenomenon before us *as* an apple, or *as* a stop sign, or *as* a balloon. When we perceive, we perceive something — *as something significant*. We always already perceive *articulated* things that are *meaningful,* due to their relationships to other things in our world and to ourselves. This seeing of something "as something" always involves an articulation of what is there and, thus, also involves an *interpretation* (*Auslegung*) of the phenomena. Our most basic experiences in the world always already involve interpretation, which means that the preinterpretive kind of pure aesthetic seeing that aesthetic consciousness is supposed to achieve is a fantasy rooted in a profound misunderstanding of what experience is really like. Seeing something *as* something is, according to Gadamer, not only always already an interpretation, but it is also always already a way of understanding. Gadamer states:

> All understanding-as is an articulation of what is there, in that it looks-away-from, looks-at, sees-together-as. . . . Thus there is no doubt that, as an articulating reading of what is there, vision disregards much of what is there, so that for sight, it is simply not there anymore. So too expectations lead it to "read in" what is not there at all. (TM, 90–91)

Because "seeing means articulating" (TM, 91), seeing means *understanding* too. Gadamer argues the same about "listening"; it too is a mode of articulating, interpreting, and understanding or "understanding-as." When we enter into a relationship with a work of art — whether by seeing, or hearing, or even reading — we are articulating, interpreting, and understanding the significance of what is before us. This means that perceiving a work of art, just like any other perception, involves a kind of *knowing* (even if this knowing is in an early or preliminary state). The depiction of our experience of a work of art in terms of the "pure seeing" of aesthetic consciousness looks from the Gadamerian point of view not only like an inaccurate account, but also a depiction of an impossibility. The assumption, built upon this picture of aesthetic experience, that our encounter with a work yields no knowledge, then, is also misguided. Gadamer concludes: "Pure seeing and pure hearing are dogmatic abstractions that artificially reduce phenomena. Perception always includes meaning. Thus to seek the unity of the work of art solely in its form as opposed to its content is a perverse formalism" (TM, 92). Aesthetic experience, like all our experience, involves our grasp of something meaningful, and involves interpretation and understanding.

What I want to point out here is that Gadamer's critique of the pure seeing of aesthetic consciousness serves also as a critique of the ideal of a preinterpretive objectivity that modern science claims to achieve. It reveals that before the scientist even approaches natural objects as the pieces of matter she wants to examine and analyze from an "unprejudiced" point of view, they are things that already have a meaningful place in the context of her world, and, thus, are always already understood and interpreted by her in some way. When a biologist studies fish, she approaches them not as strange, alien, slippery, scaly swimmers, but *as fish* that already hold a meaningful place in our world. In fact, it is the meaningful place fish already hold in our world that motivates her to study them in the first place. I take it that Gadamer is trying to get us to recognize that the preinterpretive experience or objective pure seeing, which modern science imagines itself to achieve of things-in-themselves, turns out to be an inaccurate account of understanding in any of its forms. The big lesson here is that there is a hermeneutic dimension to all experience, even the methodological experience of the natural sciences, though the natural sciences do not recognize it. (This is a key lesson that we must grasp if we are to understand Gadamer's central claims [mentioned earlier] that understanding is our very mode of being-in-the-world, and the scope of hermeneutics is universal.) All our experience, even our scientific experience, involves interpretation and meaning. Everything we see, we see *as something*. Everything we examine is already a meaningful thing that we are related to and care about in some way.

Modern science's notion of objectivity receives further criticism in Gadamer's polemical remarks regarding the methodical self-forgetting involved in historical consciousness. Here he argues that the attempt to transcend one's position in history in order to see the whole of history from a god's eye view is ultimately futile. Historical tradition, Gadamer reminds us, is not just something we aim to understand in the human sciences, but is also *something to which we always belong as human beings*. In the human sciences, then, we belong to the very thing that we are trying to understand, and we cannot treat tradition as if it were some alien object or separate thing in itself. Gadamer's reminder of the way we "belong to tradition" is directed, I take it, not only at the historical school, which has misunderstood the phenomenon of understanding that occurs in the study of history. It is also directed (again) at modern science and its conception of the sort of knowledge it believes it can attain. In presenting his insight that we always belong to historical tradition, Gadamer attacks modern science's forgetfulness of human finitude. Gadamer consistently emphasizes that we are *finite, historically situated beings* and cannot transcend this fact about ourselves. Our understanding itself (as will be discussed in part II) is always influenced by our place in history—a fact about the structure of understanding that Gadamer calls "historically effected consciousness" (*wirkungsgeschichtliches Bewußtsein*). Against the modern scientific prescription that one must rid oneself of all prejudices in order to achieve objective knowledge, Gadamer argues that all knowledge necessarily involves prejudices that are generated by the tradition to which we belong, and that prejudices (as we will also see in part II) are actually a condition for the possibility of having any understanding at all. Gadamer aims to show us how the tradition to which we belong, and the prejudgments we carry with us, form the context in which every new experience finds its sense and significance. Furthermore, he aims to show us how our presuppositions in all areas of study are what determine the direction of our investigation; for it is only out of certain pre-existing interests, questions, desires, projects, and so forth, that we inquire into anything or seek any knowledge at all. (Our fish biologist, for example, is motivated to proceed in her study, perhaps, in order to discover why the fish population is suddenly declining for a community who has depended on them as their main food source for generations.) Even the scientist, who claims to conduct her work in the spirit of "knowledge for knowledge's sake," begins with a question, a purpose, an interest that guides her examination and makes her experiments significant and worthwhile. This too is a kind of prejudgment that enables her to do her work, whether she recognizes it or not, which is just what Gadamer aims to show. He states:

> Obviously the burden of my argument is that effective history still determines modern historical and scientific consciousness; and it does so beyond any possible knowledge of this domination . . . an insight which, however, in the face of modern historical research and of science's methodological ideal of objectivity, meets with particular resistance in the self-understanding of science. (TM, xxxiv)

It is Gadamer's purpose to show us that understanding always involves *prejudgment* (*Vorurteil*) and, as we said before, *interpretation* (*Auslegung*) so that we may move beyond the exaggerated and even fantastic notions of objectivity that are rooted in a misunderstanding of how human experience truly works. Only then will we be able to recognize that the majority of our hermeneutic experience has been wrongly excluded from the realm of genuine knowledge.

THE NEED FOR A NEW CONCEPTION OF UNDERSTANDING

Having found the depictions of our experiences of art and history in terms of "aesthetic consciousness" and "historical consciousness" to be grossly incorrect (due to the various naïve and even counterproductive attempts at methodical abstraction in the name of "objective" knowledge involved in both), Gadamer sets out to correct false thinking about what happens to us when we understand and to illuminate the real experience that understanding is. This correction of false thinking is not just directed at the human sciences' self-understanding, but at the natural sciences' self-understanding as well; for Gadamer's criticism of aesthetic and historical consciousness is aimed in an important way at the fundamental assumptions of modern science in which they are rooted. Recognizing the real need for a new conception of understanding that will do justice to the genuine knowledge of genuine truth that occurs in our wide range of hermeneutic experience, including our encounters with art, text, tradition, and others in dialogue, Gadamer turns to a phenomenological study of the event of understanding.

NOTES

1. Hans-Georg Gadamer, *Truth and Method*, trans. Joel Weinsheimer and Donald G. Marshall. 2nd revised edition (New York: Continuum, 2000), xxi. Hereafter cited in text as TM, page number.

2. This is a notion of scientific method that grows out of the work of Bacon and Descartes in the early modern period, and (as Gadamer argues) remains highly influential through the thinking of John Stuart Mill and into the early twentieth century. This depiction of scientific method may appear overly simplistic today to those who are involved in current debates over methodology within the natural sciences and the philosophy of science, but it is the older depiction of method that Gadamer finds alive and well in his era and in need of confrontation. I do not mean to imply that Gadamer's project is outdated. I think, as I suggested in the introduction, that the older, narrower view of scientific method still dominates our thinking today, in spite of the more sophisticated debates that are going on in highly specialized philosophical circles. Because of this, Gadamer's critique of modern science and his project to rethink knowledge and truth beyond the confines of modern method are still relevant.

3. The modern era, for Gadamer, seems to last roughly from the seventeenth to the twentieth century.

4. Although Gadamer takes a stand against the narrow, modern understanding of "science," as that which abides by the methodological ideals of the natural sciences alone, he repeatedly uses the word "science" (*Wissenschaft*) and "scientific" (*wissenschaftlich*) in this modern, narrow sense. We need to be aware of this so that when we see him use these words in a derogatory way, we understand that it does not mean that he is criticizing science in the broader, more proper sense of "genuine knowing" that would include the work of the human sciences (*Geisteswissenschaften*) and our experience (*Erfahrung*) of the world in general. Gadamer is not "anti-science," he is against a particular, modern understanding that science has of itself.

5. The ethical aspect of treating the voice of the other in this manner will be discussed at length in part III.

6. An articulation of the unique mode of knowing involved in the human sciences had not completely disappeared, but survived in the guiding concepts of humanism (*Bildung, Sensus Communis*, Judgment, Taste), which Gadamer endeavors to rehabilitate in his own way.

7. Hans-Georg Gadamer, *Wahrheit und Methode: Grüdzuge einer philosophischen Hermeneutik* (Tübingen: J. C. B. Mohr [Paul Siebeck], 1990), 91. Hereafter cited in text as WM, page number.

8. Gadamer explains that the concept of *Erlebnis*, here, acquires an epistemological function. Dilthey is "concerned to legitimate the work of the human sciences epistemologically," and tries to find what is ultimately "given" to consciousness, just as Descartes had done in order to legitimate the natural sciences. Descartes found this "given" to be units of clear and distinct ideas. Dilthey declares that it is units of *meaning* or meaningful *experience* which constitute the special nature of "the given" in the human sciences. Experiences (*Erlebnisse*) are what is "given" to consciousness, and thus the data from which we build our knowledge of the historical world in the human sciences (TM, 65–66).

9. Gadamer explains that the concept *Erlebnis* expresses the romantic criticism of Enlightenment rationalism—an appeal to feeling and the artistic freedom to express it against cold reason, and a remembrance of our connectedness to life as a whole against the feeling of alienation brought on by modern mechanized society.

10. This way of judging aesthetic beauty, Gadamer argues, can be traced back to Kant. Kant understood the aesthetic judgment of beauty (or what he called "taste") to be based on an a priori feeling of pleasure in the subjective consciousness that accompanies the free play of the imagination and understanding incited by the beautiful object. Basing aesthetic judgment on a universal a priori feeling in the subject gave it independent validity, in that it was shown not to rely on any conceptual criteria to make its judgment. Gadamer's analysis shows that this inevitably became the basis of the autonomy of aesthetic consciousness. But, while aesthetic judgment earned its autonomy, it also lost its status as knowledge. Kant reserved "knowledge" for the spheres of theoretical and practical reason alone. Gadamer explains: "In taste nothing is known of the objects judged to be beautiful, but it is stated only that there is a feeling of pleasure connected with them a priori in the subjective consciousness" (TM, 43).

11. Gadamer identifies the turning point in aesthetics—where art gets conceived in contrast to reality—in Schiller and his influential prioritizing of the "standpoint of art" (TM, 56, 82–85). Of course, many traditional (non-Gadamerian) interpreters of the Ancients would locate the association of art with mere appearance, and not reality or truth, in Plato.

12. I want to be very clear, here, about what I take to be Gadamer's criticism of modern science. Gadamer is not saying that the modern methodological practice central to the natural sciences is inadequate for arriving at truth in the natural sciences. Gadamer recognizes the great success of the methodological practice developed in the natural sciences for discovering natural laws, predicting natural phenomena, and controlling natural objects with the use of technology. Gadamer's criticism has to do not with modern science's *practice*, but with modern science's *conception* of its practice. The first problem is modern science's conception of the scope of its methodological practice. Modern science believes that its method is the only way to reach truth, and that its method must be used any time truth is sought. (We saw how this conception was widely accepted even in the human sciences of the nineteenth century, which tried to mimic the natural science's methodological practice.) Gadamer contests this first self-conception of modern science, arguing that the modern methodological procedures central to the natural sciences are inappropriate in the human sciences, due to the human sciences' different objects and objectives of investigation. Modern scientific method is a much more limited means of arriving at truth than modern science recognizes. The second problem is modern science's conception of the kind of objectivity and truth it is able to achieve. Modern science believes it is able to achieve a prejudice-less objectivity and arrive at a noninterpretive truth. Gadamer also contests this second self-conception of modern science, arguing that all human knowledge involves prejudices, and that all human truth is interpretive, whether we recognize it or not. This is one of the deepest lessons of Gadamer's philosophical hermeneutics.

Part II

Gadamer's Concept of Play: Re-Conceiving the Process of Understanding

Chapter 2

Introducing the Key of Play

It is Gadamer's purpose in *Truth and Method* to show that there is an alternative to modern scientific method, neither inferior to, nor derivative of it, which brings forth *genuine* knowledge of *genuine* truth and has a structure all its own—a structure which must be accounted for if we are to have an accurate understanding of what knowledge and truth really are. In illuminating the problems he sees with the narrow, modern scientific conception of knowledge, Gadamer endeavors simultaneously to resuscitate the strains of thought in the history of philosophy—particularly found in Plato, Aristotle, Hegel, Husserl, and Heidegger—that help to articulate the alternative conception of understanding he wants to develop. Gadamer, as we will see, pulls together the conceptual resources available in notions like dialogue (*dialogos*), practical wisdom (*phronesis*), cultivation (*Bildung*), horizon (*Horizont*), and experience (*Erfahrung*), which express in Gadamer's view a better vision of what understanding really is; but he is still left with the work of explaining or describing at bottom how understanding, as depicted in these right-headed concepts, really works. With the phenomenological rigor, which Gadamer says, "Husserl has made a duty for us all" (TM, xxv), he describes the experience of understanding in terms of "play" (*Spiel*).

The concept of "play" is the key to understanding the real alternative to modern scientific conceptions of knowledge, method, and truth that Gadamer wants to articulate. By tracing the concept's development through *Truth and Method*, as a crucial character in the progress of the text's plot, I aim to show that "play" is a process whose relevance extends far beyond the context of art in which it is introduced, and with which it is most commonly associated in the secondary literature on Gadamer. Attending to the concept in a sustained and detailed manner will allow me to reveal "play's" global relevance in Gadamer's hermeneutics and show that "play" elucidates the very process of understanding *in general*—that understanding which stretches through all our hermeneutic experience, including our encounters with art, with text, with tradition in all its forms, with others in dialogue, and which even constitutes (as Heidegger taught) our very mode of being-in-the-world.

The concept of play inevitably depicts the structure of our fundamental relationship to the world in a way so different from the Cartesian one that has dominated philosophical thinking (all the way through Kant and the nineteenth century, according to Gadamer), that with "play" Gadamer manages to call into question all the familiar concepts of subject, object, knowledge, and truth that have been handed down to us by the early modern era. Gadamer's concept of play carries with it an implicit attack on the traditional conception of the human being as the independent "subject" who observes and knows (by making properly corresponding pictures or representations of them in his mind) the alien "objects" of the world. Gadamer carries out his attack by ultimately showing that "understanding is never a subjective relation to a given 'object' but to the history of its effect; in other words, understanding belongs to the being of that which is understood" (TM, xxxi).

In order to really grasp what Gadamer means by this, and to recognize the contrasting model of our relationship to the world that Gadamer's concept of play offers, we should first take a look at some crucial features of the Cartesian subject-object model that has come to dominate our philosophical thinking.[1]

THE CARTESIAN MODEL

Mind/Body Dualism

The Cartesian model begins with a dualism between mind and body, which also manifests itself as a mind/world, subject/object, in/out, or I/It dichotomy. In this dichotomy it is assumed that the "I," the human subject or mind, is fundamentally separated from, and stands in opposition to the "it," the alien objects, or things of the world to which even one's own body belongs. The subject and object are thought to be completely different types of things that exist independently of each other. The subject is a thinking, understanding, immaterial thing; knowledge belongs to it alone. The objects of the world are unthinking, material things that harbor within themselves some "truth" that the subject endeavors to know.[2] Subjects are those who know and act. Objects are known and acted upon. Since "I"—the thinking me—am not thought to be originally in contact with "the things" out there, the question becomes: What is my relationship to the world? *How* can I—the subject—know anything about these objects (including my own body) that are so different from me and exist apart from me?

Knowledge as Representation

A long tradition of modern epistemology answers: *Only through* the pictures or representations *in* your mind of the objects *out* there. If I am to have true, "objective knowledge" of the world, I need to have proper pictures in my head that correspond to the objects. Knowledge, then, means adequate representation *in* the mind *of* the truth of the objects of the outside world. Knowledge is a mental picture that properly maps the world.

The Edifice of Knowledge

This knowledge for which we strive is conceived as a great edifice that is constructed atomistically out of neutral units of data given to consciousness, which we accumulate and (secondarily) organize and contextualize. To ensure that I represent the truth of the world properly, I must build my pictures only out of, and on the firm foundation of, those units or ideas that I can be certain are not infected by any false assumptions or biases. To do this I must, first, bracket all my old opinions about the world (Descartes' methodical doubt[3]) and start from scratch, finding an indubitable clear and distinct idea to serve as the foundation of my knowledge (Descartes' *cogito*). I must then use as building blocks upon this foundation only other clear and distinct ideas to erect my proper picture of the world.[4]

Ethics of Disengagement

Built right into this Cartesian "method"—the method meant to ensure scientific certainty—is an "ethics of disengagement."[5] Descartes' method for knowing requires that I disengage from my old prejudices, from other people's opinions (i.e., those of society, authority, tradition), from my own interests, desires, attitudes, emotions, and even from my own body and the sensations that belong to it (for "the senses deceive"). I must do this in order to establish the clarity and neutrality of thought necessary for judging, knowing, and seeing the Truth. This "disengagement" is a familiar prescription to anyone who has attempted to achieve the status of the "objective" scientist. It is a removal or abstraction of oneself—of all of one's subjective attributes—from the investigation so that one does not interfere with it.

Monologue

If I am to achieve the clarity of knowledge prescribed by Descartes, I must abstain from projecting any of my own prejudices onto my ideas/pictures, and constrain my own judgment to accepting as true *only* what is clear and distinct by the lights of my own reason. Since, following

Descartes, I am to examine *only my own* ideas *by my reason alone* in order to discover which ones are "clear and distinct" and adequate building blocks for my secure edifice of knowledge, it is easy to see that on this model the whole "knowing" endeavor is monological. The only reliable knowledge is that which I acquire for myself independently of others. I am to silence the other voices who aim to tell me what is "true," and achieve autonomy by meditating on my own ideas with the use of my reason alone—a commandment that became the familiar clarion call of the Enlightenment: "Think for yourself."

Objective Knowledge

It is only through the discipline of abiding by these procedures of disengagement—disengagement from all those authorities except that of my own reason—that genuine, "objective" knowledge can be achieved. This is a kind of knowledge (1) that properly represents in my mind the truth of the objects in the outside world, without the interference of any subjective attitudes, emotions, biases or prejudices; (2) that is acquired by the use of my own reason alone; and (3) that is a universal knowledge, in the sense that any other rational human being by the use of the same procedures can attain it and verify it.[6]

A GLIMPSE BEYOND THE CARTESIAN MODEL

It is important to keep in mind these features of the Cartesian subject-object model in order to recognize how radically different Gadamer's notion of understanding will prove to be. In our study of Gadamer's notion of the process of understanding *as play*, we will be working to build a very different picture of the human being's fundamental relation to the world. This new picture will portray the human being not as fundamentally separate from the world, but primordially in contact with the things and people of the world. Following from this, human understanding will not be depicted as a sort of "snapshot" of the world that happens in the self-enclosed chambers of the mind, but rather as a dynamic and ongoing "event" that occurs in the process of interacting with others about what we are trying to understand. This new Gadamerian picture will reveal that *what* we understand is not a dumb, mute "object," but the meaningful subject matter (*Sache*) of a shared world that is *presented, articulated,* and *interpreted* together with others in language. It will also reveal that the truth of this subject matter is not something that resides either *in the thing* itself, or *in the mind* of the one who confronts it, but emerges *in-between* I and Thou through a joint process of presentation and recognition. Because of this, the structure of this interactive understanding will require an "ethics of engagement" (rather than disengagement), since it will emerge dialogically (not monologically) from our participation with others in conversation. We will come to realize, finally, how differently the human being's relation to the world looks in the Gadamerian picture when we see the human being not as a spectator at a distance from the world, nor as a subject standing over and against the world, but as a dialogical creature who is an engaged being-*at-play*-in-the-world with others.

NOTES

1. This analysis of the Cartesian subject-object model of knowledge is based on Descartes' *Meditations on First Philosophy*, translated by John Cottingham (Cambridge: Cambridge University Press, 1986).

2. Descartes, *Meditations*, "Sixth Meditation," 54.

3. Descartes, *Meditations*, "First Meditation."

4. I do not mean to neglect the important role that God plays for Descartes in our acquisition of knowledge of the world. According to Descartes, we cannot even be certain that the outside world, independent of our own thoughts, exists at all without the (clear and distinct) notion of a perfect God, the proof of his existence, and the certainty that this being would not be a malicious one who means to constantly deceive us. Mind and matter are, for Descartes, then, not the only existing things in the universe. In fact, neither would exist without the simultaneous presence of God.

5. This is a phrase Charles Taylor commonly uses in his lectures on what he calls "mediational epistemology."

6. Even with Kant's Copernican revolution—where knowledge is no longer thought to be of the (noumenal) "thing-in-itself," but of the phenomenal world, whose order is not (passively) discovered by us, but (actively) constituted by us through the projection of our categories of understanding on it—the knowledge that we are able to achieve is still thought to be "objective," universal knowledge *in* the mind *of* the phenomena *out*side. Kant, then, remains a part of the Cartesian tradition in crucial ways.

Chapter 3

Understanding Art: The Play of Work and Spectator

"All encounter with the language of art is an encounter with an unfinished event and is itself part of this event."

—Gadamer's *Truth and Method*, 99

In *Truth and Method*, Gadamer introduces the concept of "play" in his description of the "event" of understanding that occurs in the experience of a work of art. Gadamer had found this experience inadequately depicted by modern aesthetics in terms of the abstraction procedures of "aesthetic consciousness." As we saw in chapter 1, aesthetic consciousness empties out the artwork of its truth by treating it as a purely formal object that exists in its own aesthetic world, detached from any reality that could be "knowable." Having declared that aesthetic consciousness fails to express the unique mode of knowing involved in the encounter with art, Gadamer sets out in the first part of *Truth and Method* to do justice to the real experience (*Erfahrung*) of a work of art, and offer a phenomenological account of the genuine knowledge of genuine truth that takes place in this experience. In the encounter with art, Gadamer finds artwork and spectator to be participants in a continuous to-and-fro play of presentation and recognition in which meaning is communicated, and a shared understanding of some subject matter takes place.

Throughout his description of our encounter with art, Gadamer moves us away from envisioning the artwork as a static object whose essence is hidden deep inside of it, and the spectator as a subject who watches from a distance and has no affect on the essence of the work. Instead, Gadamer aims to show us how the spectator plays a crucial interpretive role in what the meaning of the artwork is. He aims to show us how it is only in the back and forth play of communicating meaning between presenter and spectator that interpretive understanding occurs and the artwork achieves its completion. Art, then, must be understood not as a "thing" that exists independently of any audience, but as part of an event in which meaning is communicated and a shared understanding is reached. Gadamer maintains that "the work of art is not an object that stands over against a subject for itself. Instead the work of art has its true being in the fact that it becomes an experience that changes the person who experiences it" (TM, 102). Gadamer also aims to move us away from the notion that understanding is something that happens within the enclosed chambers of the subject's mind, disengaged from the "objects" it tries to know. Instead, Gadamer teaches us to recognize how understanding itself only takes place in a dynamic, interactive, interpretive process of working through meaning with others. A shared understanding is in this way an interpretive event that takes place in a play of presenting and recognizing meaning.

THE MOVEMENT OF PLAY

In introducing the concept of "play" (*Spiel*) Gadamer tells us immediately that when he uses the word it is not in the subjective sense found in Kant and Schiller. Play is not something that happens in the mind or the impulses of the subject.[1] It is not a subjective act or attitude, but is, rather, an activity that always goes on *in-between* the players and reaches beyond the behavior or consciousness of any individual player. Play has a life, essence, or spirit of its own that emerges from the players' engagement in their to-and-fro rhythm. Gadamer explains that in the activity of playing, the players become absorbed in a dance of mutual responsiveness that takes on a unique pattern, and that it is this pattern of movement (*Bewegungsordnung*) that becomes the meaning or the "subject matter" (*die Sache*) of play. He states: "The players are not the subjects of play; instead play merely reaches presentation (*Darstellung*) through the players" (TM, 103). It is the game itself (*das Spiel selbst*) that is the subject or subject matter of the play, and this game has the character of an "event" (*Geschehen*). Play, then, is fundamentally something larger than the individual player or his mental state; it is a pattern of movement that surpasses the players, and is something to which both players *belong*.

Crucial to Gadamer's notion of play as an "event" is that it is a *process* whose character is fundamentally *dynamic*. Gadamer perceives that what is essential to the definition of "play"—as seen in our use of the word when we speak of everything from the play of light, waves, or colors to the play of gears, forces, or words, and so on—is the spontaneous back and forth movement (*Bewegung*) that continually renews itself. Because it is the occurrence of this movement that constitutes play, it is not even necessary for there to be what we would properly call playing "subjects"—purposive human beings—for play to take place. For instance, play is something we also see in nature—in the instinctive wrestling of animals, in the dance of wind-blown leaves, in the melodic ping of raindrops, and so forth—where there is no intentional behavior involved. In fact, Gadamer declares that we should say, strictly speaking, not that nature plays "like us," but that, insofar as the human being is a part of nature, "*man* too plays. His playing is a natural process" (TM, 105). This is a point Gadamer reiterates in his 1973 essay "The Play of Art," where he presents play as a phenomenon that truly blurs the line between man and other animals. Here he calls play "an elementary phenomenon that pervades the whole of the animal world and . . . determines man as a natural being."[2] In fact, Gadamer suggests, there is something about the movement of play that is essential to all living things—an insight to which we will have occasion to return in chapter 9. But for now, what is important is that the very "happening"[3] of the movement is what is essential to play—a movement that emerges, as said, *in-between* the players, not inside any one of them.

Because the back-and-forth movement is so essential to play, we can see that play itself cannot be a solitary event. The movement of play itself requires (at least) two. There must be a respondent for the motion to continue and the game to go on. Gadamer states:

> The movement to-and-fro obviously belongs so essentially to the game that there is an ultimate sense in which you cannot have a game by yourself. In order for there to be a game, there always has to be, not necessarily literally another player, but something else with which the player plays and which automatically responds to his move with a countermove. Thus the cat at play chooses the ball of wool because it responds to play, and ball games will be with us forever because the ball is freely mobile in every direction, appearing to do surprising things of its own accord. (TM, 106)

As Gadamer's example of the ball indicates, another important feature of the movement of play is that it is a movement that is essentially variable, and has a certain *freedom* to it. This means that it cannot be fully determined or mechanical, but involves the possibility of spontaneity and variety. For the movement of play to occur, then, there must be room reserved for the freedom of variability—a variability that can only take place if the players' moves are not identical to each other or totally predictable in advance. We can see already from this brief sketch of play that it is a process that is fundamentally dynamic, interactive, and variable in a way that relies on the engagement between things or players that are *different* from each other.[4] If the process of understanding meaning, which Gadamer insists occurs in our encounter with art, is itself a kind of play-event, then we should not expect to find this process locked inside any one of the players, for instance as a set of mental procedures or patchwork of images in the brain. We should, rather, expect to find the process developing *in between* different players as a shared experience that depends upon both players' contributions.

HUMAN PLAY

Gadamer observes that it is only in the movement of play (*Spielbewegung*) that the unique pattern or "subject matter" (*Sache*) of play "presents itself," or shows itself. Gadamer calls "self-presentation" (*Selbstdarstellung*) "a universal ontological characteristic of nature" (TM, 108) of which man is a part; but he also makes an important distinction between *human* play and the play of the rest of nature. Gadamer perceives that what is peculiar about human play, is that it

> plays *something:* That means that the structure of movement to which it submits has a definite quality which the player "chooses." First, he expressly separates his playing behavior from his other behavior by *wanting* to play. But even within his readiness to play he makes a choice. He chooses this game rather than that. (TM, 107)

Human play is not simply instinctive, nor caused by some outer force (as with the play of leaves in the wind), or the result of some coincidental combination of things (as with the play of colors in a field), but involves the *intention* or the *choice* to constrain one's own freedom to the rules of a game. It involves the *willingness* to enter into a particular game of one's choosing, where one restricts one's own actions to the performance of the tasks proper to the game.[5] In his 1977 article "The Relevance of the Beautiful," Gadamer even says that

> the specifically human quality in our play is the *self-discipline* and order that we impose on our movements when playing, as if particular purposes were involved—just like a child, for example, who counts how often he can bounce the ball on the ground before losing control of it. . . . In this fashion we actually intend something with effort, ambition, and *profound commitment.*[6]

Human play, then, has the special quality of *human* freedom, which is not simply the freedom of variability, or the freedom of caprice; but it is a freedom that involves the intentional self-restraint that goes along with any effort to accomplish *something*, do *something*, play *something*.

It is in performing the tasks that we set for ourselves in play that we present the subject matter of play. But, furthermore, Gadamer tells us that it is in performing the tasks of play that we also present *ourselves*. In play, the human being "plays himself out."

> The self-presentation of human play depends on the player's conduct being tied to the make-believe goals of the game, but the "meaning" of these goals does not in fact depend on their being achieved. Rather, in spending oneself on the task of the game, one is in fact playing oneself out. The self-presentation of the game involves the player's achieving, as it were, his own self-presentation by playing—i.e., presenting—something. (TM, 107–8)

This suggests that it is only by presentating *something else*, in the back-and-forth movement of playing a game, that a human being is able to present his/her self. Gadamer, here, begins to give us a hint as to the far-reaching significance of our participation in games. Here we get a first sense that our *being-present* or *being-here* is intimately wrapped up with *being-a-participant* inside some world, some community with others in which we attend to the presentation of something beyond ourselves, that is, the subject matter of our worldly experience. This is in stark contrast to the Cartesian model where *being-here* means first and foremost *being present-to-myself-alone* in my own mind as a thinking thing, and second *being separate-from-the-world* of objects that I observe.

In continuing to move beyond the Cartesian emphasis on self-consciousness, Gadamer emphasizes the *"primacy of play over the consciousness of the player"* (TM, 104). He describes play as having an active life of its own, of absorbing the players into itself, of holding the players in its spell, and of drawing them into the game. As Gadamer describes it, play is less of a thing a person does, and more of a thing done to him—or, better, an event in which one becomes caught-up. Gadamer declares that "all playing is a being-played . . . the game masters the players" (TM, 106). The order of the game itself leads the players, which Gadamer describes as giving the participants a feeling of ease, lightness, and freedom from the burden of taking the initiative. I do not think, though, that we should regard these comments as being in tension with the previous emphasis on the intention, choice, willingness, and self-discipline involved in human play. We should not conclude from these remarks that the players somehow become quite passive in play, but rather that they become a part of an activity that is bigger than their own personal, active roles in it. This is exactly what happens anytime we become truly "interactive." Here, the players allow the play to take priority over any individual part they may perform and give themselves over to the movement that is taking place. They "lose themselves" in the game that envelops them, but with the seriousness of a fully engaged participant—for, as Gadamer observes, "Seriousness in playing is necessary to make the play wholly play. Someone who doesn't take the game seriously is a spoilsport" (TM, 102). Here again, I want to emphasize the *active* side of play that is always driving what may sometimes sound like its passive characterization. Though the game, of which the player is just a part, may surpass him or subsume him, taking priority over his individual role, it remains essential to the existence of the game that the player actively *conduct himself* in his playing in such a way that he, with full seriousness and involvement, attends wholeheartedly to the tasks required of him.[7] Gadamer states: "A person playing is, even in his play, still someone who comports himself, even if the proper essence of the game consists in his disburdening himself of the tension he feels in his purposive comportment"[8] (TM, 107). To put this another way, one cannot truly participate in play in a half-committed manner or from a distance—the kind of distance, for instance, one might maintain in approaching "play" as a kind of *thing* that is "just a game." When one does this, when one objectifies the game by looking at it from the outside while he means to be participating in it, he creates space between himself and the game and takes himself out of true involvement in play. The mode of being of play, instead, demands that the players be completely *engaged* with other players *in* the game.

Once again, if the process of understanding meaning, which Gadamer insists takes place in our encounter with art, is a kind of play-event, then this understanding will require that the players be willing to get actively involved in the game in a serious way. What it takes to fully engage in the game of understanding, what exactly the character of our proper "comportment" in this kind of play is, and what tasks we must commit ourselves to accomplishing in this kind of play will be filled out further in the discussion (below) of the role of the participating spectator in the encounter with art, and even more so in the upcoming chapter on the ethical conditions of play (chapter 5). For now, it is worth noting that truly engaging in any kind of human play requires a particular kind of behavior or *conduct* on the parts of the players, and the achievement of certain tasks. For the game to really take place, the players must *commit* to the game and behave as genuine participants .

THE EMERGENCE OF THE WORK OF ART AND THE PRESENTATION OF TRUTH

Human play reaches its ultimate consummation, according to Gadamer, in the work of art. The process through which this consummation takes place he calls "transformation into structure" (*Verwandlung ins Gebilde*). Taking up the example of performance art, Gadamer explains that "transformation into structure" occurs when the activity in which the players are involved is directed toward an audience or spectator—that is, when their presentation becomes a *representation of something for someone*. The players now participate in their play in such a way that their roles serve to generate a meaningful whole (*Sinnganze*), which is offered to a spectator and is meant to be recognized by him. It is the *directedness* of the players' activity toward an audience that distinguishes the play of art from the ongoing patterned activity of playing we have considered so far. In opening up to the spectator the movement in which the players are involved, playing now becomes "a play," showing becomes "a show."

It is the movement, which is just getting started in-between the show and the spectators, that is crucial to our study. The presentation of a meaningful whole to an audience sparks the beginning of a new activity of play—the back-and-forth communication of meaning, or interpretive play, which constitutes the process of understanding. The players in this new game are (on the one hand) the whole performance comprised of the individual actors and their intermingling movement, and (on the other) the audience members wrapped up in the show, going through the story being performed, and bearing witness. It is through the back and forth movement of presenting and recognizing meaning that a shared understanding develops. This understanding, according to Gadamer, is nothing less than a shared *knowledge of truth*.

But what does art have to do with truth? We have already heard Gadamer argue that the artwork does not simply pull us into some fantasy realm of mere appearance, but rather teaches us something about our common world and creates for us an opportunity for knowledge. But how does this work? In one of his most cryptic moments in *Truth and Method*, Gadamer declares that the transformation into structure of art is also the "transformation into the true" (*Die Verwandlung ist Verwandlung ins Wahre*) (TM, 112; WM, 118). We must grasp Gadamer's vision of the relationship between art, reality, and truth if we are going to grasp how our play-encounter with art can legitimately be considered a mode of understanding in which we come to know some truth.

According to Gadamer, a work of art has a special relationship to "being." It is what Gadamer calls an "ontological event." Gadamer explains that in the work of art *what is* (*was ist*) appears meaningfully and visibly. Art "brings to light what is otherwise constantly hidden and withdrawn" (TM, 112). In the transformation that occurs when the work of art emerges, "being" (*Sein*) is "brought forth";[9] but it is brought forth in a way that it is transformed into the structure that Gadamer calls "a superior mode of being." In art, being is brought forth and "raised up"[10] into its truth! This likely sounds rather abstract, but what Gadamer is getting at here is that in every artistic presentation there exists an *articulation* of our reality, of world, or of some subject matter to which we all (in principle) have access. This articulation involves pointing to something, illuminating something in a particular way, or showing something *as something specific*, so that it can be seen clearly and meaningfully by us. Articulating involves highlighting certain aspects of a thing, leaving others out, and, thus, offering an interpretation so that, as Gadamer puts it, "the being of the representation is more than the being of the thing represented, Homer's Achilles more than the original" (TM, 114). Taking up this example, Achilles (the man) may already exist in our world before the artwork is made, but with Homer's help he is pointed out and given definition. In art, Achilles' character is shaped and highlighted and he is transformed into *Achilles the greatest of all warriors*. This is what Gadamer means when he says that what is represented in art "is there" (*Das Dargestellte ist da*), but in art it is brought forth so that it may "come into the There more authentically" (*eigentlicher ins Da gekommen ist*) (TM, 114; WM, 120). In art what "is there" gets *articulated* so that it can be seen *as it is*. In every work of art, Gadamer maintains, there is just this kind of attempt to say something about our world, emphasize some aspect of our reality, and claim "this is *how* it is." When a work of art presents some articulated subject matter to us, it makes what Gadamer calls a "claim to truth" (*Wahrheitsanspruch*).

This claim to truth is only the first move in the play of understanding. The very fact that the work of art "brings forth" some articulated subject matter implies a "someone for whom" it is brought forth. The artwork addresses us and awaits a response. When the artwork makes a claim to truth, it intends for its articulation of the way the world looks to "ring true" to us. The artwork means for its articulation to be *received* (i.e., *interpreted*) by its audience *as the way things are*. Gadamer refers to this kind of reception as "recognition" (*Wiedererkennung*). The artwork aims for its articulation of truth to be recognized by us, and when we do recognize what the artwork presents to us, we finally reach the experience of knowledge that Gadamer has insisted takes place in our encounter with art. Gadamer explains: "In recognition what we know emerges, as if illuminated, from all the contingent and variable circumstances that condition it; it is grasped in its essence. It is known as something" (TM, 114). It is only once the recognition[11] of truth takes place by an audience that the achievement of communication that Gadamer calls "total mediation" (*totale Vermittlung*)[12] occurs. The total mediation of meaning is what allows the work to become fully "present" to us or, as Gadamer puts it, "contemporaneous" so that it may "live" in our world. It is only in the total mediation of meaning that the work of art reaches its completion and the phenomenon of play we've been tracing finally has "the character of a work, or an *ergon* and not only of *energeia*. In this sense I call it a structure (*Gebilde*)" (TM, 110).[13] The transformation into structure that completes the work of art and allows truth to reach presentation, we can now see, depends upon that process of presentation and recognition, that movement of showing-as and seeing-as, that dynamic joint articulation of being, to take place. The transformation into structure and presentation of truth, in other words, is rooted in that process of communicating meaning that we have been describing as the game of understanding.

THE PARTICIPATION OF THE SPECTATOR: THE COMMITMENT OF THE ENGAGED PLAYER

The total mediation or full communication of meaning that allows for the transformation into structure to take place requires something that we began to see glimpses of in our discussion (above) of human play: the commitment of the engaged player. In the game of understanding, which artistic presentation sparks when it offers up a meaningful whole to an audience, the spectators are crucial players. A true spectator of an artwork is not one who simply happens to be in the room in a quite casual way while the performance is going on; rather, he must *participate*. His participation involves what Gadamer calls "a subjective accomplishment in human conduct" (*eine subjektive Leistung menschlichen Verhaltens*) (TM, 125; WM, 130). The spectator has a task to fulfill. He must devote his full attention to the articulated subject matter before him, and become completely involved in interpreting the truth-claim presented to him. The spectator's task is to *lend* himself to this truth, and allow its claim to be made upon him. Gadamer explains that lending ourselves to the meaning presented to us in art means becoming caught up in the performance and allowing ourselves to be carried away by it. This description echoes Gadamer's earlier characterization of the serious player in any game, who must become totally involved so that the spirit of the game guides him. He must "lose himself" in the game. When one accomplishes the task of becoming "caught up" in the performance, one reaches a state of, as Gadamer calls it, "being outside oneself" (*Außersichsein*). Gadamer states: "Being outside oneself is the positive possibility of being wholly with something else" (TM, 126). Being outside oneself, in a very basic way, means opening yourself up to something "other" than yourself and allowing it to affect you. This "opening up" to meaning "other" than your own is crucial if any common understanding is to be reached. The distance involved in "being outside oneself" that the true spectator must achieve is not the distancing from oneself that was necessary for aesthetic consciousness. That was a distancing in which one tried to abstract all considerations of meaning and truth from the encounter with the artwork. It was a distancing, thus, in which one tried *not to participate* with the artwork out of a fear of infecting one's experience with nonaesthetic elements. The *true* aesthetic distance of which Gadamer speaks is a distance that does not preclude participation. It is the distance, as he puts it, that is "necessary for seeing, and thus makes possible a genuine and comprehensive participation in what is presented before us" (TM, 128). It is also, as we will see, a distance that neither separates us from ourselves, nor divorces us from our world, but enriches our understanding of the world and sense of belonging to it.

Gadamer directs us to the quintessential example of the way the spectator of an artwork shares in the meaning presented to him when he turns to the encounter with a tragic work of art. In the encounter with a tragic work of art the spectator undergoes an experience in which he comes to an enhanced knowledge and self-knowledge. Gadamer begins his discussion by drawing on Aristotle's famous definition of tragedy, which includes (as an essential part of its definition) the effect tragedy has on the spectator. For Aristotle, tragedy has the effect on the spectator of pity (*eleos*) and fear (*phobos*). But, as Gadamer argues, these are not to be conceived of as "subjective" or inner states of mind of the spectator. Rather, they are

> events that overwhelm man and sweep him away. . . . *Eleos* is the misery that comes over us in the face of what we call miserable. Thus we commiserate

with the fate of Oedipus . . . *phobos* means the shivers of apprehension that
come over us for someone whom we see rushing to his destruction and for
whom we fear. (TM, 130)

In watching a tragedy the spectator experiences—or in a profound way
undergoes —the tragic events *along with* the characters. Gadamer states:
"Commiseration and apprehension are modes of *ekstasis*, being outside
oneself, which testify to the power of what is being played out before us"
(TM, 130). But this "being outside ourselves," this ecstatic "self-forgetfulness" that makes it possible for us to become involved in what the artwork
is presenting to us, does not just tear us away from ourselves. It returns us
to ourselves in the very moment we grasp the meaning presented; for
recognizing *the truth* in what is presented to us means at the same time
recognizing ourselves. But how is this so? Gadamer explains that in the
tragic events being presented to us on stage, there is a claim to truth made:
"It is the disproportionate, terrible immensity of the consequences that
flow from a guilty deed" (TM, 132). In our recognition and affirmation of
the tragedy's truth—that is, not that the tragic events are "just," but that
they are *the way things are* and make up some sort of world order in which
we too live—we recognize ourselves as bound to the same truth and the
same tragic fate as the hero before us.

Our total immersion in the play-process of understanding that takes
place in our experience with the tragic work of art involves both a
distancing from ourselves and a return to ourselves—a return to our *new,
transformed* selves, who now more profoundly grasp the world and our
place in it. We should recognize, here, that our newfound, enriched
understanding and self-understanding could never have occurred without our interpretive interaction with *something other* than ourselves, some
new meaning offered to us by another. Recognizing this helps us see that
truth, or an understanding of truth, is not something one can simply come
upon through disengaged armchair philosophy—as our modern predecessors may have taught us. It develops, rather, only in our engaged
participation, our back and forth *play*, with something or someone beyond
ourselves.

We should also recognize, and much more clearly now, why Gadamer
had argued earlier that art should not be regarded as *mere* appearance in
opposition to reality. As Gadamer shows us, art is the articulation of
reality so that it may appear and be grasped in its truth. This is the case,
Gadamer argues, whether art is conceived in terms of representation, or in
the classical terminology of imitation (*mimesis*).[14] The representation or
imitation involved in art are both a matter of bringing forth real being and
articulating it in its truth, which means that *knowledge* already belongs to
both representation and imitation. Gadamer states: "When a person
imitates something, he allows what he knows to exist and to exist in the
way that he knows it" (TM, 113). Representing and imitating are them-

selves *modes of knowing,* and our recognition of what the other knows and shows us—that "subject matter" or "being" that is brought forth and articulated for us as its truth—is a way of joining in on that knowing. Now that we can see that, as Gadamer puts it, "art is knowledge and experiencing an artwork means sharing in that knowledge" (TM, 97), we can also see that the experience of art cannot be reduced to the feeling of pleasure or entertainment. It is rather a profound and enriching experience (*Erfahrung*)[15] in which we are transformed. In the experience through which we recognize the subject matter that has been brought forth, articulated, and presented to us in art, we are not adrift in a fictional fantasy world, but are becoming more connected to the real world in which we always live. Gadamer explains that our experience of art "is not enchantment in the sense of a bewitchment that waits for the redeeming word that will transform things back to what they were; rather, it is itself redemption and transformation back into true being" (TM, 112). Our play-encounter with art, then, is an event of shared knowing in which some subject matter is articulated and raised up to its truth. We can without qualms, then, conceive of our play-encounter with art not as just some sort of play of "feeling," but as a play of *understanding.*

BEYOND DRAMA: UNDERSTANDING THE PLASTIC ARTS

We have seen how the artwork cannot be conceived as a simple object, or "thing in itself," but must be seen as a part of a process in which meaning is communicated. The artwork really only reaches its completion in the activity in which articulated subject matter is presented and recognized as truth—that is, in the play-process of understanding. Envisioning art at first in terms of drama is particularly helpful in Gadamer's exposition, since it is easiest for us to see that a dramatic stage-play's existence as a work of art cannot be separated from its performance for an audience. The same fact can easily be recognized of music. "A drama really exists only when it is played, and ultimately music must resound" (TM, 116). In these cases, the work of art lives each time it is presented and represented in new and different ways to new and different audiences throughout the ages. But Gadamer claims that this fact about drama, music, and the other performing arts is true for *all kinds of art.* He states: "The work of art cannot simply be isolated from the 'contingency' of the chance conditions in which it appears, and where this kind of isolation occurs, the result is an abstraction that reduces the actual being of the work. It itself belongs to the world to which it represents itself" (TM, 116).

It may have been relatively easy to agree with Gadamer, that an artwork's life is really fulfilled only in the play-process of its presentation to an audience in which its meaning is understood, when the type of art we were considering was performance art; but it becomes more difficult to follow him when we consider an artwork that seems much more like an unchanging thing, such as a painting or a sculpture. According to Gadamer a painting or a sculpture is what we generally call a "picture" (*Bild*), which *seems* to exist independent of any performance or presentation: "Such pictures apparently have nothing about them of the objective dependence on mediation that we emphasized in the case of drama and music" (TM, 135). Any variations in people's encounters with these sorts of artworks *seem* to be in the mind or life of the subject—subjective variations which aesthetic consciousness would simply abstract in order to see the work objectively, or "in itself." In the case of a picture, then, doesn't the artwork exist simply as an object, while any understanding of its meaning exists separately in the mind of the subject? If we are to describe our encounter with a picture, mustn't we be thrown back to a classic Cartesian portrayal of the way a subject knows an object? Does understanding really have the same sort of interactive play-structure in the experience of a picture as it did in the experience of a drama?

Gadamer argues that the "picturing" plastic arts have the same mode of being as the performing arts—that of presentation. Just as the presentation of meaning in the performing arts depended on the participation of the spectator and his recognition of what was brought forth and articulated, we find that in the plastic arts as well the participation of the viewer is crucial if the picture's meaning is to be communicated, and if the picture is going to be "brought to life." The picture, just like a drama, can really only exist as a work of art in the play of presenting and recognizing what is in the picture. The picture can only reach completion in the play-process of understanding its truth.

But, one might ask, what does a picture have to do with truth? Isn't the picture just a copy of the truth? Isn't the picture fundamentally removed from what is real, and so removed from truth? Gadamer is quick to reply to these old prejudices about art, and he sets out to show us that the "picture" actually does the same work we saw in the performing arts. The picture, just like the stage-play, brings forth "being," articulates it, and raises it up to its truth. The relationship between a picture, reality, and truth must be established if we are to recognize that our encounters with the plastic arts, like our encounters with the performing arts, involve genuine understanding of genuine truth.

In Gadamer's discussion of the performing arts we saw an "ontological interwovenness of original and reproduced being" (TM, 137), where a presentation and a representation of a tragedy, for instance, were not "copies" of an original, copies of copies, or unreal dreamlike images, but were, rather, *the appearance of the original in its articulated truth.* This constituted what Gadamer called an "ontological event." Gadamer explains:

The world that appears in the play of presentation does not stand like a copy next to the real world, but is that world in the heightened truth of its being. And certainly reproduction—e.g., performance on the stage—is not a copy beside which the original performance of the drama itself retains a separate existence. The concept of mimesis, applied to both kinds of presentation, did not mean a copy so much as the appearance of what is presented. Without being imitated in the work, the world does not exist as it exists in the work. It is not there as it is there in the work, and without being reproduced, the work is not there. (TM, 137)

Gadamer argues that the same is the case with the "picture," whose mode of being is also presentation and which should also *not* be conceived as a "copy."[16] The picture too is an ontological event in which being appears.

To help us understand the difference between the presentation of a picture (*Bild*) and the repetition of a copy (*Abbild*), Gadamer shows us how the picture and the copy are related differently to the original (*Urbild*). The copy has "no other task but to resemble the original" (TM, 138) and identify it so that it is recognizable to us (as in a passport photo or picture in a sales catalog). In doing this it does not attract attention to itself in its own separate being, but tries as much as possible to disappear in pointing away from itself toward what is copied. It does not try to say anything specific about the original, or show it in a particular light, but simply to repeat it. In this way, the copy remains simply dependent on the original for its existence as mere repetition, and has a one-way, or one-sided, relationship with it. The picture, on the other hand, just like the representation of which we spoke in the performing arts, is not a mere repetition, but a bringing forth and an articulating of the original so that it is present *as* something—so that it is present *as its truth*. The picture is not self-effacing like the copy, but invites our attention to *how* it represents the thing it does—that is, to its particular *interpretation* of the subject matter. It makes a meaningful claim to truth about some subject matter that it asks us to recognize and understand. And this is the key to the distinction between picture and copy, for a copy does not try to *articulate* the original at all. The copy makes no claim.[17]

The picture becomes much more than a copy. Whereas the copy remains simply dependent on the original, the picture on the other hand achieves a life of its own. As an interpretation, articulation, and meaningful presentation of something—as a meaningful claim to truth—the picture exists as something unique in itself and, thus, has its own being. This does not mean that it loses all connection with the original, for it *belongs* to the original, inasmuch as the original remains the subject matter that is articulated in a particular way in the picture, and inasmuch as the picture is one of the original's possible self-presentations or manifestations. To express the way the picture "belongs" to the original, Gadamer calls the self-presentation of the picture an *emanation* of the original, or an overflow through which the original experiences an "increase in being"

(TM, 140). The picture "shares in the mysterious radiation of being that flows from the being of what is represented, what comes to presence there" (TM, 149). We can see here the "ontological valence" (as Gadamer calls it) of the picture, for—as an emanation and manifestation of the original, or as an appearance of its being—it *shares in the being* of the original. The original is brought forth in the picture so that it is there for us to see.

Now, as we remember from our previous discussion of the performing arts, any "bringing forth" of being implies a "someone for whom" it is brought forth. The picture, like any other work of art, points something out to us, shows it to us in a particular way, and waits for our recognition. The picture too makes a claim to truth, and awaits a response. We can see this in the way a portrait (a particular kind of picture), offers a particular articulation of someone who it expects its audience to recognize. The viewers of the portrait, just like the spectators of a drama, will have to actively participate with the portrait's presentation if they are going to recognize the person being presented, or more accurately, recognize the truth that is claimed about that person depicted (for instance, that a particular man depicted was brave or noble). The viewers, then, must commit to engaging in that to-and-fro movement of presentation and recognition that we have seen is necessary for a shared understanding of meaning to take place. What we have seen here is that the understanding of truth that takes place in our encounter with the plastic arts has the same structure of play that we saw in our encounter with the performing arts. Even in the plastic arts we must conceive of the work of art not as an object in itself (*ding an sich*), but as a part of an event of communication that is completed only through the participation of the committed spectator. Even in our encounter with the plastic arts we must conceive of the understanding of meaning not as something that takes place inside the mind of the subject, like the formation of a mental image of some external object, but as an interactive event of presentation and recognition.[18]

UNDERSTANDING LITERATURE: INTRODUCTION TO THE PLAY OF THE TEXT AND THE READER

It is in Gadamer's final discussion of our encounter with the literary work of art that we are raised to a broader view that allows us to examine understanding as it occurs in the work of the human sciences as a whole. This takes us one step closer to being able to see how the process of understanding in general, and thus *all* hermeneutic experience, is a play-process.

Just as a drama found its life only in its performance for an audience, and the picture in its presentation for the viewer, Gadamer claims that "it is just as true that literature—say in its proper art form, the novel—has its original existence in being read" (TM, 160). In the literary artwork, just as with any other work of art, we find an articulation of some aspect of our reality, and a claim to truth that is offered to an audience for recognition. This literary work depends on the reader for its meaning to achieve total mediation, for it is only through being read with understanding that the "truth" presented by the text can be communicated and shared. Here we see, again, how the participation of the audience in the play-process of understanding is crucial for the work of art's completion. The reader belongs to the concept of literature, just as much as the spectator belongs to the concept of the drama, and the viewer belongs to the concept of the picture.

Literature, for Gadamer, serves as an important borderline concept that allows us to cross over from our discussion of art alone, and the play-structure of our hermeneutic experience with art, to a discussion that includes the mode of knowing involved in the work of the human sciences as a whole. This is because, as Gadamer declares, "literature" does not just include the literary work of art.

> All written texts share in the mode of being of literature—not only religious, legal, economic, public and private texts of all kinds, but also scholarly writings that edit and interpret these texts: namely the human sciences as a whole. Moreover, all scholarly research takes the form of literature insofar as it is essentially bound to language. Literature in the broadest sense is bounded only by what can be said, for everything that can be said can be written. (TM, 162)

What we have discovered about literature in the narrow sense of the literary work of art applies also to literature in this broad sense, according to Gadamer. It is not only the literary work of art that makes a claim to truth that can only achieve meaningful presence when it is understood by some reader; all writing tries to communicate something significant to us that we want to grasp, and whose meaning cannot live without being grasped by us. Gadamer states:

> Just as we were able to show that the being of the work of art is play and that it must be perceived by the spectator in order to be actualized (*vollendet*), so also it is universally true of texts that only in the process of understanding them is the dead trace of meaning transformed back into living meaning. (TM, 164)

Differences in literary form do not change this fact. It is *what* the text tries to say to us that we are trying to understand and, thus, it is the *content* that is significant to us—regardless of whether we are reading a novel, poem, essay, report, or any other piece of writing. Because of this, we are concerned less with the differences in form, and more with the differences in the claims to truth that are made or, in other words, the differences in meaning. Gadamer states: "Literary art has in common with all other texts the fact that it speaks to us in terms of the significance of its contents. Our understanding is not specifically concerned with its formal achievement as a work of art but with what it says to us" (TM, 163). In this case—and this is a major point for Gadamer—the kind of encounter we have with a work of literary art in which we come to understand its meaningful content is not so different from the encounter a historian, philosopher, or other type of human scientist has with any sort of text. When we begin to make this connection, we start to see that the play-process of understanding that we have described in our encounter with art is the same sort of process we experience in our encounters with texts of all kinds.

NOTES

1. A brief history of the term "play" in aesthetics, as Gadamer understands it, is as follows: Gadamer explains that for Kant, aesthetic judgment or "taste" is based on an a priori feeling of pleasure in the subjective consciousness brought on by the "free play" of the cognitive powers (of the imagination and the understanding). This free play is encouraged by the internal coherence of form of beautiful objects (or, rather, the internal coherence of form *is enough* to incite the free play of the cognitive faculties, and produce the feeling of pleasure upon which our judgment of its beauty is based. No concept or purpose in the beautiful object is needed to incite this in us). Taste possesses universal validity because it is based—not on private sensual preference, from which taste in fact abstracts—but an a priori element that is common to all; thus, critique in matters of aesthetics is possible. According to Gadamer, through Kant taste (1) becomes radically subjectivized (based on a "feeling" in the subject rather than a sense of appropriateness cultivated by living in one's society), (2) is restricted to the realm of the beautiful or aesthetics (from its wider domain of social matters—aesthetic and moral—in general), (3) becomes a judgment independent in its validity (not limited by intellectual or moral criteria), and (4) simultaneously loses its status as knowledge (since nothing is *known* of the beautiful object through taste, but it is judged based on its form alone). Consequently knowledge becomes restricted in Kant to the theoretical and practical use of reason (TM, 42, 43). Schiller, Gadamer tells us, picks up Kant's notion that taste is based on the free play of the cognitive faculties, reinterprets it in terms of Fichte's theory of impulses, and turns it into a demand: the play instinct (that harmonizes the form instinct and matter instinct) *must be cultivated*, which is the goal of aesthetic education (TM, 82).
2. Hans-Georg Gadamer, "The Play of Art" in *The Relevance of the Beautiful*, ed. Robert Bernasconi (Cambridge: Cambridge University Press, 1986), 123.
3. Gadamer points out that the close connection between "play" and "happening" comes out clearly in German phrases such as "something (e.g., a movie) is playing (*spielt*) there" or "something is going on (*im Spiele ist*)" or "something is happening (*sich abspielt*)" (TM, 104).
4. This will be important to remember when we face a discussion of Gadamer's critics, who claim that his hermeneutics is fundamentally antagonistic to difference. In our study we see early on that difference is the lifeblood of the play-movement in which, we will see, understanding takes place.
5. I do not want to suggest that humans *always* engage in this kind of intentional play, but that only humans *are able* to play in this way.
6. My emphasis. Hans-Georg Gadamer, "The Relevance of the Beautiful" in *The Relevance of the Beautiful*, ed. Robert Bernasconi (Cambridge: Cambridge University Press, 1986), 23.
7. It is true that Gadamer locates "play" in the back-and-forth movement that occurs in-between the players, and not in the intentional consciousness of any one of

them. And yet, as I am arguing here and as we will come to see more fully in chapters 4 and 5, such a genuine movement cannot occur unless the players actively comport themselves in such a way that they become fully involved or immersed in the game. Drew Hyland, in his book *The Question of Play* (Lanham, Md.: University Press of America, 1984), argues that Gadamer denies the intentional character of play, and that for him "play simply 'happens' to the player independently of his or her intentions" (88) and further that "the attitude of the player has nothing to do with whether or not there is play" (89). I think this depiction misses a crucial aspect of play. Though the players' intentions and attitudes are not the locale of play, no play can take place without (what we might call) seriously playful attitudes and intentions. As chapter 5 will show more clearly, the players' shared comportment toward each other and toward the game is a crucial condition for the possibility of any genuine play at all. Though it cannot be fully developed here, I would venture to say that Hyland's own articulation of play as involving the "stance of responsive openness" actually shares much more in common with Gadamer's notion of play than he recognizes.

8. "Comportment" is a translation of *Verhalten*, also meaning behavior or conduct.

9. The "bringing forth" of being that occurs in art is a translation of *Hervorholung*—a getting of something out of something, a producing of something from something. This "bringing forth" of being reveals the ontological significance (*Seinssinn*) of art or representation (*Darstellung*), which Gadamer is so eager to defend against the idea that art is a fictitious world of appearance separate from reality.

10. The "raising up" referred to here is a translation of *Aufhebung*, which does not entail a simple cancellation or destruction of a previous state so that a new one can emerge, but rather a "going beyond" that is a possible development only through the collection and preservation of what came before. Now we can see that art is both a "bringing forth" (*Hervorholung*) of being and a "raising up" (*Aufhebung*) of this being into its truth in the play of presentation and recognition.

11. Notice, here, that the proper response to art, which constitutes our "grasp" of it, is not to *feel* it—to *feel* the aesthetic pleasure its form inspires, as Kant had suggested. Rather, the proper response is to *recognize* some *truth* in it—to *understand* and to *know* its meaning. That recognition (*Wiedererkennung*) is the way in which we grasp an artistic representation (*Darstellung*)—or a "bringing forth" of being—reveals that our experience of a work of art has cognitive significance (*Erkenntnissinn*) and is a mode of knowing.

12. The concept of mediation (*Vermittlung*) holds a special place in hermeneutics, since Hermes himself, after which this "art of interpretation" is named, was the mediator, or "go-between" enabling communication between mortals and gods. In mediation two things that were previously separate are brought together so that they are in contact with each other, so that they communicate with each other, so that they are meaningfully present to one another. The communication of the artwork's meaning is a matter of achieving contemporaneity through a mediation between past and present.

13. We should notice, here, that the audience is by no means irrelevant to the emerging work of art and its meaning, as if it were a merely passive observer. On the contrary, the audience is an integral *part of* the show and actually completes the work. The audience's active role of *recognizing* what is being presented is essential to the movement of communication in which the work of art finds its life in the world.

14. One of Gadamer's philosophical missions, it seems, is to properly educate us as to the true meaning of *mimesis*, and to help us to see that imitation does not represent the relationship between an original and a copy (which is discussed in greater detail in the coming section on the plastic arts). *Mimesis* is, rather, a showing of something *as* something so that the truth of what one is trying to show shines through and can be identified and recognized by us. For a particularly good and brief articulation of this point, see Gadamer's essay "The Play of Art" in *The Relevance of the Beautiful*, 128–29.

15. Gadamer uses the word *Erfahrung* to indicate the transforming sort of experience in which we come to *know* something new about *our reality* and ourselves. This is in

contradistinction to the word *Erlebnis* that we saw used by modern aestheticists to indicate a very personal experience, largely characterized by feeling, which overflows into the artistic expression of one's own personal life.

16. Gadamer here is addressing the long tradition in aesthetics of conceiving of art as copies, copies of copies, or "third removed from the truth"—a certain strain of thought coming out of Plato.

17. This is also what distinguishes a picture from a sign or symbol, neither of which articulate or make a claim about some subject matter. The copy, the sign, and the symbol are not *artistic* representations for this reason. They are not works of art (TM, 151–55).

18. This is an important point because the more the piece of tradition we are trying to understand seems like an "object," the easier it is for us to slip back into thinking that the old Cartesian or natural scientific model of knowledge will apply. But Gadamer wants to show that even a piece of tradition that is object-like (such as a sculpture or man-made artifact) cannot be treated like a natural object because it tries to say something to us—it tries to articulate something to us—that we must interpret. The old subject-object model of knowledge cannot work in this case, because understanding what the piece of tradition has to say requires that we enter into a communication with it. This communication will follow the same play-process we've been describing all along.

Chapter 4

The Play of Interlocutors:
Understanding as Dialogue

In his phenomenological account of our encounter with a work of art, Gadamer has described work and spectator as players and participants in a continuous to-and-fro movement or dance of presentation and recognition, out of which the meaning of the work of art emerges and is understood. Gadamer's introductory discussion of play has deserved special attention because it has laid the groundwork for grasping the process of hermeneutic experience in general. Through Gadamer's discussion of art we have seen an exemplary account of how understanding is something that "happens" only in the movement of our back-and-forth interpretive engagement with what we are trying to understand. In our discussion of art we have found early clues to unlocking the meaning of Gadamer's distinct conception of understanding. It is, as Gadamer declared in his introduction, "never a subjective relation to a given 'object'" (TM, xxxi) as the Cartesian model (upon which modern science was built) would have it. It is, rather, a dynamic, social, multivocal process of engagement in which we move beyond the nearsightedness of our own individual perspective, and toward more universal points of view that enrich our grasp of the world and ourselves in it.

In Gadamer's discussion of understanding texts and the shift to the kind of understanding that occurs in the human sciences as a whole, the field of "hermeneutics" is finally introduced for the first time in *Truth and Method*. Hermeneutics is the classical discipline concerned with the art of interpreting texts, specifically religious and literary texts. In contrast to the narrow focus of hermeneutics in the classical tradition, Gadamer envisions the proper territory of hermeneutical efforts to be quite broad. He claims:

> Everything that is no longer immediately situated in a world—that is, all tradition, whether art or the other spiritual creations of the past: law, religion, philosophy, and so forth—is estranged from its original meaning and

depends on the unlocking and mediating spirit that we, like the Greeks, name after Hermes: the messenger of the gods. (TM, 165)

The work of hermeneutics, for Gadamer, involves the effort to understand any and all kinds of tradition (*Überlieferung*), making hermeneutics the work of the human sciences in general.[1] Expanding on what we learned in Gadamer's discussion of art and text—that our encounters with artworks and texts are "events" of interpretation, or play-processes of presenting and recognizing meaning in which a shared understanding is reached—Gadamer now argues that the same is true of our encounters with *any* and *all* forms of tradition. He states: "Understanding must be conceived as a part of the event in which meaning occurs, the event in which the meaning of all statements—those of art and all other kinds of tradition—is formed and actualized" (TM, 165).

THE HERMENEUTIC CIRCLE AND THE PLAYING-OUT OF PREJUDICES

Gadamer explicates the process in which we understand tradition more fully when he turns to his discussion of Heidegger's contribution to the "hermeneutic circle."[2] What I want to show here is that Gadamer's presentation of Heidegger's contribution to the hermeneutic circle is itself a richer and more detailed description of what happens in the play-process of understanding.

The old hermeneutic rule for understanding texts—that the meaning of the whole must be understood in terms of its parts, and the parts in terms of the whole—is transformed by Heidegger in a unique way. Heidegger shows us that the "circle" out of which meaning emerges is not just a formal one that takes place, for instance, within the text itself (as if the text's meaning were self-contained in the circular relationship between its whole and parts). It is a circle that takes place between *us, our* historical horizon or context of meaning, and that of the text. Heidegger's description of the circular movement in which we "work out our fore-structures in terms of the things themselves," shows us how it is that we become aware of and revise our expectations of the meaning of that form of tradition we are trying to understand. It is in and through this hermeneutic circle that the mediation between past and present (which Gadamer has declared takes place in all understanding) occurs.

The mediation between past and present is what Gadamer famously refers to as a "fusion of horizons" (*Horizontverschmelzung*). What I want to point out here is that the back-and-forth process of working out our fore-projections (*Vorentwurfe*) or fore-conceptions (*Vorbegriffe*) of meaning, in which a fusion of horizons takes place, is itself another articulation of that ongoing movement of play (between text or artwork and audience) that constitutes the fundamental process of all understanding. In fact, Gadamer himself states that the hermeneutic circle "describes understanding as the interplay [*Ineinanderspiel*] of the movement of tradition and the movement of the interpreter" (TM, 293; WM, 298). This characterization of the hermeneutic circle as the movement of play is too often forgotten because of the popular fascination with the image of fusion, which (as I mentioned in the introduction) is the focus of critics who claim that Gadamer's notion of understanding is fundamentally antagonistic to "difference" among viewpoints. Fusion, to these critics, means that one horizon of meaning overtakes another so that any distinction between them is lost. The point that I want to make, here, is that if we understand what Gadamer really means by "fusion" in terms of its larger context of the play-process, then we can avoid believing that Gadamer's conception of understanding is one that tries to—to put it bluntly—"kill difference." Here I want to show that fusion, in its proper context of the interplay of tradition and interpreter, is just another way in which Gadamer attempts to describe understanding as the sharing of a common game—a game of articulating a common subject matter together, and a game in which there remains an ongoing, open-ended movement between different players and their contexts of meaning.

Heidegger's exposition of the circle illuminates how, in our encounter with what we want to understand (whether it be a text, or other form of tradition), we always bring with us a set of prejudgments (*Vorurteile*) or expectations about the meaning we will find. These prejudgments make up the "fore-structure" of the understanding. As one reads a text, for instance, prejudgments of meaning are projected in a provisional or anticipatory way on the text and are tested. One projects the meaning of the whole, and the text either confirms or resists one's expectation of meaning. This either results in an enriched understanding of one's initial judgment of meaning, or sparks a process of revision in which one becomes aware of one's mistaken assumptions and tries out a new modified interpretation.

Gadamer emphasizes that the prejudgments of which Heidegger speaks are an integral part of all occurrences of understanding and are, in fact, the condition for the possibility of any understanding at all. Prejudices, to Gadamer, should not be conceived simply as negative entities, as they have been defined by the Enlightenment. They should not be taken to be merely false, blinding, unfounded judgments. A prejudice originally meant, Gadamer's analysis shows, "a judgment that is rendered before all the elements that determine a situation have been finally examined" (TM, 270). It is only due to the Enlightenment's "prejudice against prejudice"—which asserts that "the only thing that gives a judgment dignity is its having a basis, a methodological justification (and not the fact that it may actually be correct)" (TM, 271)—that prejudice becomes a purely negative term. The Enlightenment takes prejudices to be primarily those judgments handed down to us by the authority of tradition, an illegitimate authority that it aims to override with the proper authority of pure reason. The influential discrediting of prejudices that we find in modern science (which claims to rid itself completely of all prejudices and achieve unbiased neutrality and objectivity) has its roots, Gadamer argues, in this Enlightenment project. More specifically, it finds its roots in the Cartesian project that only admits as credible and certain those ideas that can in no possible way be doubted. But for Heidegger and Gadamer our prejudices or prejudgments have the positive function of making understanding possible. They are the provisional or anticipatory judgments that are initially projected, and subsequently go through a process of revision that is guided by the subject matter one is trying to understand.

For Gadamer, it is right to associate prejudices with the particular tradition into which we are born, and which is handed down to us. The fact that we are influenced by tradition through our prejudices, though, is for him not objectionable, but rather a fact of human life. Gadamer stresses that all human beings are finite, historical beings that find themselves situated in (or *thrown* into) a particular tradition, or a particular point in time in the ongoing development of tradition, which shapes their under-standing of things. For Gadamer, this indicates something of primary importance about the structure of understanding in general. All under-standing is influenced by our own place in tradition and is a historically effected event. All consciousness, as Gadamer puts it, is "historically effected consciousness" (*wirkungsgeschichtliches Bewußtsein*). The tradition to which we belong offers us the terms in which we initially understand new things, and forms the *horizon* of understanding with which we always start when we encounter something new.[3] Our horizon is that background understanding or the context of meaning in which we integrate new experiences. Our prejudices are the expression of this horizon, and "constitute the historical reality of [our] being" (TM, 277). The prejudices we have at any one time "constitute, then, the horizon of a particular present" (TM, 306). The influence of our historical tradition upon our thinking in the form of prejudices is, according to Gadamer, not something we can eliminate, nor is it something we would want to erase. It does not hinder our achievement of genuine knowledge, but rather makes the process in which we come to such genuine knowledge possible by providing us with a context in which we can make at least some preliminary sense of new experiences.

Being born into a tradition means being born into a meaningful world of things and people—a home in which we share a basic familiarity with the *subject matter* whose truth we are working to explicitly understand through our interactive communication with the text, the work of art, or some other form of tradition. So, not only is tradition our object of investigation in the human sciences, it is also something we are connected to and *belong* to as historical beings. Work and interpreter—both belonging to tradition—find themselves in a continuous world of meaning, and it is because of this *belonging* that the interpreter is able to recognize the subject matter that the work articulates in its unique way. Gadamer declares that we must recognize that "a person seeking to understand something has a bond to the subject matter that comes into language through the traditionary text and has, or acquires, a connection with the tradition from which the text speaks" (TM, 295). The fact that we have a previous bond to the subject matter, provided by our own orienting tradition, allows us to recognize what the work is talking about. The underlying point here is that the work we encounter is always something that is at once strange to us (in its particular claim) and familiar to us (in the subject matter about which it makes a claim); but without the familiar part, the strange part could not become intelligible. "Hence the most basic of all hermeneutic preconditions remains one's own fore-understanding, which comes from being concerned with the same subject" (TM, 294). This fore-understanding (*Vorverständnis*), provided by our own orienting tradition, takes the form of what Gadamer calls "enabling" prejudices. These enabling prejudices make new understanding possible first by anticipating meaning in advance, and then subsequently by being tried, tested, or "worked out" so that the revision necessary for us to improve our understanding can take place.

We have seen here that prejudices in themselves are not necessarily bad or a hindrance to our understanding. They, rather, have a productive function of enabling the possibility of any understanding at all. What we need to guard against in our efforts to understand, then, is not prejudice per se, but allowing our prejudices to go unchecked, untested, or untried. We need to guard against our understanding being dominated and ruled by our preconceptions alone. Gadamer declares (appropriating Heidegger) that "all correct interpretation must be on guard against arbitrary fancies and the limitations imposed by imperceptible habits of thought, and it must direct its gaze 'on the things themselves'" (*die Sachen selbst*) (TM, 266). This is the "constant task" of the interpreter. Here we hear Gadamer's old description of play and the player's commitment reverberate. In play the players must lend themselves to, and let themselves be led by, the subject matter itself (*die Sache selbst*). That we must guard ourselves against arbitrariness in our interpretation, and guard against the tyranny of our prejudices, ultimately means here that we must guard against dropping out of play. It is only in and through our engaged play-process with the text or work of art that our presuppositions come to the fore so that we become aware of them explicitly, have the chance to adjust them, and improve our understanding. Thus, we must make sure that we keep ourselves in play so that we keep our prejudices in a process in which they get checked. This is the only way to guard against the tyranny of prejudices over our understanding.

To be clearer, we saw that the assumptions or presuppositions with which we begin make up a kind of background of understanding, which we always carry with us. Our prejudices form a context of meaning in which we integrate new experiences. But this background of understanding usually goes unnoticed. It is only through our experience of some new meaning that resists or denies our projected presuppositions, that these presuppositions become foregrounded in a way that we can become aware of them, examine them (their origin and validity), and transform them so that the understanding we have of the subject matter is improved—so that we "know better." Gadamer says that foregrounding (*abheben*) is the "way prejudices are brought into play" (TM, 306). Being brought into play means that they are provoked out of the unnoticed background of our constantly operating assumptions, and brought to the table so that they are tried or, better, *risked*—a risking which means opening up the possibility that they may be wrong. Risking our prejudices means making them questionable and suspending their validity. The provocation which brings our prejudices into play can only be accomplished through our engagement with *something else* or *someone else* that asserts his or her own meaning and validity. It is our engagement with new meaning, then, that we will need to preserve in order to inevitably improve our understanding. What is demanded of us as interpreters, then, is not that we

> forget all our fore-meanings concerning the content and all our own ideas. All that is asked is that we remain open to the meaning of the other person or text. But this openness always includes our situating the other meaning in relation to the whole of our own meanings or ourselves in relation to it. (TM, 268)

Our work as engaged interpreters, in which we bring our prejudices into play and risk them, relies fundamentally on a conduct of *openness*.

This openness, Gadamer tells us, means being prepared for the text to tell us something and being sensitive to its alterity.

> A person trying to understand something will not resign himself from the start to relying on his own accidental fore-meanings, ignoring as consistently and stubbornly as possible the actual meaning of the text until the latter becomes so persistently audible that it breaks through what the interpreter imagines it to be. (TM, 269)

Instead, a person trying to understand something must be ready to hear something different from what he already thinks, allow otherness to assert itself, and become aware of his own biases (TM, 269). Openness means letting the traditionary text or work of art *speak to us, address us, affect us,* and even *transform us* in our thinking. It requires standing, then, with our ears open and *listening*. This readiness is not the stance of neutrality, nor the attempted erasure of prejudices that we find in scientific consciousness. To stand back as a disengaged observer is *not* to risk oneself or one's presuppositions. It is to *keep oneself out of play*. Gadamer makes an important point about the project of staying out of play when he says: "This is the demand of science" (TM, 335) or, in other words, the demand of modern scientific method. Gadamer consistently shows us that understanding demands the opposite. Understanding is only possible if one keeps oneself *in* play. The demand of modern scientific method, as we discussed early on in chapter 1, is based on a profound misunderstanding of what makes understanding possible, and hinders the process in which we can come to understand meaning. If the process of understanding is going to get underway, we must not keep ourselves at a distance, but *open* ourselves to strange and different meaning and actively *engage* it. We must bring our own presuppositions to the table and risk them. If we want to understand, then, we'd better participate and *get in the game*! The concept of play, here again, reveals itself to be the key to grasping the real alternative to the modern scientific conception of understanding that Gadamer is trying so hard to articulate.

THE FUSION OF HORIZONS AND THE INTERPLAY OF PAST AND PRESENT

Because understanding is affected by the prejudices that reflect our place in history and the tradition to which we belong, Gadamer describes our understanding as the "furthering of an event that goes far back" (TM, xxiv). But this does not mean that we are locked into the views of our forefathers and are determined to understand things as they did; for, whatever prejudices we have that are informed by the particular traditionary understanding handed down to us, as we have seen, are constantly being worked out, confirmed, denied, and revised through *our* encounters with the subject matter. This process of revision is how the tradition handed down to us gets transformed in a way that applies to the world in which we currently live. The way *we* understand things need not be—and, in fact, will not be—the same as the way our predecessors did, because our experiences, interests, and concerns, in which the meaning handed down by tradition will find its relevance for us, are different from our predecessors' experiences, interests, and concerns. Therefore, as Gadamer states, "We understand in a *different* way, *if we understand at all*" (TM, 297).[4] Take, for instance, the way we might understand a traditionary text. Our understanding of it will not be the same as that of the original author, original readers, or even our teachers because the text will have a new relevance for us that relates to our current issues. It will apply to our own situation differently than it applied to theirs. A contemporary reader of Plato, for instance, might find much more significance in the role that gender plays in the dialogues than readers of previous generations did.

This is because of the different social climate in which we live—a climate that finds historical and contemporary claims about men and women worthy of examination in the quest for social justice. Through different readers' understandings, interpretations, and appropriations over time, the meaning of a Platonic text itself emerges anew in different and surprising ways. Its truth undergoes a continual, endless process of unfolding, as it proves to bear in new ways on new audiences. But our own new understanding must be conceived as growing or developing out of a history of understanding that came before, and not as a kind of knowledge achieved from outside of tradition altogether, or apart from all prejudices; for this would be an impossibility for historical beings such as ourselves. The way to properly think of our own understanding is as a transformation, revision, or *appropriation* of traditionary understanding that is handed down to us. Understanding is, to use Gadamer's famous phrase, a "fusion of horizons" (*Horizontverschmelzung*). He states:

> The horizon of the present is continually in the process of being formed because we are continually having to test all our prejudices. An important part of this testing occurs in our encountering the past and in understanding the tradition from which we come. Hence the horizon of the present cannot be formed without the past. There is no more an isolated horizon of the present in itself than there are historical horizons which have to be acquired. *Rather, understanding is always the fusion of these horizons supposedly existing by themselves.* (TM, 306)

This fusion of past and present horizons in which tradition is appropriated, Gadamer argues, is the very *movement and life of tradition itself.* Tradition cannot live without the contemporary interpreter who understands it anew.

The appropriation, mediation of past and present, or fusion of past and present horizons that is accomplished in the play-process of understanding reveals to us that *application* (*Anwendung*) is always an essential part of understanding. Gadamer argues: "In the course of our reflections we have come to see that understanding always involves something like applying the text to be understood to the interpreter's present situation" (TM, 308). It is only in finding the relevance of what is articulated in tradition, for our own time, that its meaning can live for us and truly be understood.[5] Understanding (*Verstehen*), interpretation (*Auslegung*), and application (*Anwendung*), Gadamer argues, are three intertwining elements of the same hermeneutical process. The process of understanding always involves the task of application, which overcomes the temporal distance between historical text, or the work of art, and its audience. The process of application is what overcomes the alienation of meaning that a separation in time has produced, so that a living relationship between work and interpreter can be accomplished.[6]

It is important to emphasize here that, just because our understanding of a text or artwork changes over time, with its changing relevance and applicability for us, this *does not mean* that its meaning simply submits to whatever meaning we project on it. There is what Gadamer calls a "fluid multiplicity of possibilities" (TM, 268) of meaning that can emerge from the text. But this does not mean that the meaning can be just anything, or whatever I arbitrarily decide. Gadamer will not allow for this sort of "anything goes" relativism in interpretation. Even though there might be a plurality of good, valid, or "correct" interpretations of a text, this does not mean that there are no bad, invalid, or incorrect interpretations. Bad interpretations are certainly possible. How do we know this? We know it because we all experience the phenomenon that takes place if we consistently misinterpret the meaning of a particular word, concept, phrase, or story in the text. We will inevitably meet some conflict or contradiction in the text that will cause us to rethink our interpretation, and go through the process of revision already mentioned as a necessary process in the circular movement of understanding. This experience teaches us that the text *will resist bad interpretations.* Because of this experience we know that, though there may be a plurality of correct interpretations of meaning, not all interpretations are correct. As long as this is the case we can speak of some kind of objectivity in interpretive understanding, which for Gadamer can be defined as "the confirmation of a fore-meaning in its being worked out" (TM, 267). Objectivity is not the removal of, or attempt to forget, all our fore-meanings, which modern science convinces itself is possible. Correct interpretation and true understanding is achieved when the meaningful whole that one projects onto the text is finally (after a long back-and-forth process of trial, error, and revision) confirmed by all the details. Gadamer states:

> The anticipation of meaning in which the whole is envisaged becomes actual understanding when the parts that are determined by the whole themselves also determine this whole. . . . The harmony of all the details with the whole is the criterion of correct understanding. The failure to achieve this harmony means that understanding has failed. (TM, 291)

Understanding, as we have seen, means engaging and participating with the meaning that is presented to us—that is, not standing back as a kind of observer, but bringing ourselves into a hermeneutic circle which is "the interplay [*Ineinanderspiel*] of the movement of tradition and the movement of the interpreter" (TM, 293; WM, 298). It is in this interplay that the mediation, or fusion of past and present horizons occurs, and meaning lives for us in a new and relevant way.

We must take a moment and probe further into the meaning of this famous image of "fusion," since it is the topic of such great interest and criticism among Gadamer scholars. As I mentioned in the introduction, the world has come to associate Gadamer's notion of understanding with a "fusion of horizons." It is not only emphasized in every introduction to Gadamer, but it is heavily dwelled upon by his critics. The image of fusion appears to many of Gadamer's critics to destroy difference among ideas in a way that is ultimately oppressive and does violence to otherness, alterity, or resistance.[7]

Consider, first, Jürgen Habermas's critique of Gadamer. In his "Review of *Truth and Method*,"[8] Habermas states: "In Gadamer's view, ongoing tradition and hermeneutic inquiry merge to a single point. Opposed to this is the insight that the reflected appropriation of tradition breaks up the nature-like [*naturwüchsige*] substance of tradition and alters the position of the subject in it."[9] Here Habermas reveals his reading of, and his worry about, the notion of understanding as a fusion of horizons; for here he *opposes* what he calls a "merging" of the past and of our understanding of the past, to "reflective" (or "critical") appropriation. He envisions that "merging" means a kind of absorption of one horizon of meaning into another, into "*a single point,*" where there is no room for differing or criticizing, and no freedom from the powerful authority of the dominating horizon of tradition. In other words, Habermas sees the fusion of horizons, which Gadamer argues takes place in all understanding, to be a kind of unification that involves the submission of one horizon to another—in this case, the submission of our present horizon to that of the past. He, thus, charges Gadamer's hermeneutics with "cultivating prudence" in a way that "shifts the balance between authority and reason,"[10] and makes reason yield to the authority of tradition.

In rehabilitating prejudice, Habermas believes that Gadamer has forgotten the oppressive power of tradition, from which the Enlightenment tried so hard to break free with the independent use of reason. He says of Gadamer that he not only is "convinced that authority need not be authoritarian,"[11] but also he has denied reflection its ability to reject the claims of tradition and break up dogmatic forces.[12] Because Habermas believes that the work of hermeneutics is driven only by what he calls (in his lecture "Knowledge and Human Interests"[13]) a "practical cognitive interest," and has as its goal simply "the preservation and expansion of the intersubjectivity of possible action-orienting mutual understanding"[14]—or what he refers to as "consensus"—he restricts its domain to a sort of *noncritical* interpretive understanding of meaning. In contrast to the "historical-hermeneutic sciences," Habermas argues that the "critical sciences" are driven by an "emancipatory cognitive interest" and, thus, are "concerned with going beyond this goal to determine when theoretical statements grasp invariant regularities of social action as such and when they express ideologically frozen relations of dependence that can in principle be transformed."[15] According to Habermas, the power of reflection, which is utilized in these critical sciences, is able to cut through the uneven power relations or relations of oppression that are handed down to us in a way that hermeneutic interpretation is not. He, thus, insists that "the right of reflection demands that the hermeneutic approach restrict itself. It calls for a reference system that goes beyond the framework of tradition as such; only then can tradition also be criticized."[16] Because the domain of hermeneutics does not offer a space beyond tradition from which a critique of tradition could occur, but instead always interprets from within the bounds of tradition, Habermas holds that hermeneutics must recognize that it does not and cannot cover the territory of all understanding. There is a kind of critical understanding, from Habermas's perspective, that hermeneutics is just not capable of. Because hermeneutics simply cannot achieve an appropriate amount of critical distance, hermeneutics must, according to Habermas, recognize its limits. This means, ultimately, that Gadamer must recognize that his claim that the domain of hermeneutics is "universal"—that hermeneutics as a theory and practice of interpretation has such a broad scope that it refers to the understanding of all meaning—is not true.

Now, whereas we find with Habermas the concern that the fusion of horizons means a submission of our present horizon to the past, and a kind of understanding which leaves no room for critique, we find with other critics a somewhat opposite concern that fusion means our simple assimilation of the past in which we make it our own and do away with its otherness. In this case, the concern is that our understanding of tradition or the traditional text becomes far too much a reflection of ourselves, instead of a reflection of its author's original meaning. Consider the concerns of an early critic of Gadamer's *Truth and Method*, Emilio Betti. Betti's worry, as expressed in his "Hermeneutics as the General Methodology of the *Geisteswissenschaften*,"[17] is directed also at Gadamer's notion that tradition and the knowledge of tradition "constitute a unity," and that understanding tradition for Gadamer means "entering into the process of tradition in which past and present constantly mediat[e] each other."[18] In other words, Betti's concern is also directed at the problem of the fusion of past and present horizons. Betti feels that Gadamer's notion that prejudice is a *condition* of understanding leads to a loss of objectivity in interpretation—not in the sense of the interpreter's submission to tradition (as we saw with Habermas), but rather in the sense of his subjective projection of meaning onto tradition or the traditionary text.[19] Betti believes that hermeneutics must articulate a set of methodological rules that, if followed, will guarantee the validity of our interpretations— or, more specifically, that will guarantee that we preserve and represent the original meaning of the author in our understanding. He finds in Gadamer's utter lack of method a deficiency in any real criterion for correctness in understanding. Gadamer's notion that understanding always involves the interpreter's "expectation of meaning" (however much it is tested and revised) appears exceedingly subjective and relative to Betti. The meaning that is finally understood in the Gadamerian model looks too much like the interpreter's own meaning or his own projection for Betti's taste, especially when Betti believes that the meaning that is understood should be that of the author. Betti states:

> The obvious difficulty with the hermeneutical method proposed by Gadamer seems to lie, for me, in that it enables a substantive agreement between text and reader—i.e., between the apparently easily accessible meaning of a text and the subjective conception of the reader—to be formed without, however, guaranteeing the correctness of understanding; for that it would be necessary that the understanding arrived at corresponded fully to the meaning underlying the text as an objectivation of mind. [20]

A Gadamerian fusion of horizons, from Betti's point of view, appears to mean that the interpreter's horizon overtakes that of the traditionary author so that the author's meaning is lost. In Betti's contrary view, "the interpreter should be content to comprehend and accept the differing opinion of the text as something different." [21] We can find a similar kind of concern in those critics who, taking their philosophical inspiration from Derrida, charge Gadamer's notion of understanding-as-fusion as one that works to diminish the difference or alterity of meaning present in the expressions one is trying to understand. [22] I want to address these critics more closely in the next chapter, where the ethical dimension of their charges will be more obvious; but for now it is worth mentioning that the popular phrase "fusion of horizons" is commonly interpreted and criticized as meaning the submission of one horizon to another, where the outcome is either a dominating past or a dominating present.

The critics' concerns about Gadamer's notion of understanding as a fusion of horizons are important ones. They reveal to us the problem of power that we must recognize is always a potential problem when we endeavor to develop a shared understanding. Any time we are trying to understand what a text, artwork, or other form of tradition says to us, we run the risk of either accepting the traditional meaning in a wholly uncritical way and allowing it to dominate our minds, or projecting our own meaning onto tradition and twisting it to say what we want it to say. The problem in both cases is the problem of a dominating power suppressing difference or a diversity among ideas. A diversity of ideas is something that we experience as a crucial contribution to any sort of inquiry into truth. One idea cannot be challenged or checked if different ones are not heard. If diversity is suppressed, if debate is silenced, we run the risk of that tyranny of prejudices that we mentioned earlier. There is a further problem of power here that these critics reveal to us. Any time we attempt to reach a shared understanding, there is not only the danger of one voice silencing the others or out-shouting them so that they cannot be heard. There is also the danger of one voice actually putting words in the other's mouth, and thereby doing a kind of violence to the individuality of the Other and his own thought. This is a way of misrepresenting what the Other says, and doing him an injustice in the process. What I want to show here, in my defense of Gadamer against his critics, is that Gadamer too is worried about these important problems, and aims to give an account of genuine understanding that does not fall prey to them.

Let's start with the way Gadamer conceives of our connection to tradition. We remember that Habermas was concerned about the way that Gadamer sees us as always bound to tradition, so that tradition informs the way we understand new things, and even informs the way we look back and view what tradition has to say to us through its texts, artworks, and so forth. Habermas is worried that in this scenario we are never able to get the distance from tradition that would enable us to critique its messages. This would result in the power of tradition having an oppressive unchecked hold on our thinking. If this is the case—if a hermeneutical understanding of tradition means merely submitting to what it tells us, and never really being able to break conceptually with it—then hermeneutical understanding cannot be the only kind of understanding (as it claims to be when Gadamer says that the scope of hermeneutics is universal). In such a case, there must be another kind of understanding that is capable of critique, and we'll have to leave hermeneutics behind if we want to understand tradition in a way that does not amount to simply adopting its views. What I want to show here is that Gadamer does conceive of hermeneutical understanding as involving the possibility of critique so that tradition's domination over our thinking is avoided.

For Gadamer, tradition is something that we are originally thrown into, belong to, and always remain within in a way that informs our current understanding of things. Habermas is right to see this connection between our thinking and tradition. But this does not mean, for Gadamer, that tradition has a chokehold on us, or that it holds us captive so that we cannot critique it. Tradition is not just something we belong to, but is also something that *belongs to us*. It is always being reworked and modified by us, which is in fact the way it is *kept alive*. In this case, "tradition is not simply a permanent precondition; rather, we produce it ourselves inasmuch as we understand, participate in the evolution of tradition, and hence further determine it ourselves" (TM, 293). Tradition lives only through our continued understanding of it, which always means (as we have seen) our *different* understanding of it and *appropriation* of it, in which we accomplish the task of mediating past and present. In this case, "fusion" means that we learn to see the relevance of past meaning in light of our current situation, which involves not just adopting past meaning, but evaluating it in reference to our current world. A fusion of horizons does not, then, mean that we leave our own horizon of meaning behind and take on the horizon of the past.

With this thought in mind, we can see, in response to Betti, why "fusion" also can't mean a simple assimilation of past meaning to our own, so that it no longer contains anything different or strange from which we might learn something new. We remember that Betti was worried that Gadamer's notion of fusion would amount to the interpreter projecting his own meaning onto the text, or putting his expectation of meaning into the author's mouth, so that the author's original meaning is lost. It is important to see, though, that Gadamer too is worried, like Betti, about the problem of projecting one's own prejudices onto the text so that the interpretation becomes totally subjective. This is why Gadamer reminds us that for true understanding to occur "it is constantly necessary to guard against overhastily assimilating the past to our own expectations of meaning. Only then can we listen to tradition in a way that permits it to make its own meaning heard" (TM, 305). For Gadamer: "Every encounter with tradition . . . involves the experience of a tension between the text and the present. The hermeneutic task consists in not covering up this tension by attempting a naïve assimilation of the two but in consciously bringing it out" (TM, 306). Gadamer, thus, knows that true understanding cannot amount to the projection of the interpreter's meaning onto the text, which is why his notion of understanding as a fusion of horizons demands the ongoing revision process of the interpreter's prejudices. But Gadamer will fundamentally disagree with Betti that the real meaning of the text must be equivalent to the author's original intention. (This is a position of Gadamer's that will become clearer when we discuss his debate with Schleiermacher in chapter 5.) Gadamer argues that an artist's articulation, once it has been made, takes on a life of its own in the world so that its range of meaning spans beyond the intentions or interpretations of its maker. Its meaning will emerge in and through its interaction with its audiences, unfolding in new ways to new audiences. Its meaning may take on a significance to a particular era of spectators that its author could never have anticipated. Meaning, for Gadamer, must be conceived (as we have shown) as "shared" meaning that emerges in-between presenter and audience through an interpretive play-process of presentation and recognition. So, though Gadamer shares and tries to anticipate some of Betti's concerns in his description of the way the process of genuine understanding works, Gadamer's notion of correct interpretation is fundamentally different from Betti's. For Gadamer, correct interpretation cannot be reduced to knowing what meaning the author intended, but encompasses the scope of all the possible meanings that the artwork may speak to any number of audiences. The danger that Gadamer does guard vigilantly against is the danger that understanding as a fusion of horizons will ultimately mean the domination of one horizon by another. We must remember that appropriating tradition and accomplishing the "fusion" of horizons requires *"participating in an event of tradition*, a process of transmission in which past and present are constantly mediated" (TM, 290). This process of transmission is one in which past and present find themselves in a relationship where they are both contributing participants. This *interactive* relationship cannot, then, amount to the reader simply acting upon a passive text in order to make it say what he wants or imagines it to say. This is something we understand best when we put "fusion" back into its context of the play-process of understanding, where subjective interpretations are always tested and revised by an ongoing interaction with the text that (we might say) "pushes back" or "talks back" when we interpret incorrectly.

If we are to grasp Gadamer's unique notion of understanding, then the phrase "fusion of horizons" that he uses to describe this understanding must be considered in terms of the larger play-process of which it is a part. It must be understood in terms of the dynamic, ongoing "sharing" of a common game—that game of developing a joint articulation of truth—in which we find an *interplay* of traditionary meaning and a contemporary interpreter, or an *interplay* of past and present horizons. The play-process, as we saw, always involves *different* players with their *different* horizons, which cannot become identical if the movement of the game is to go on and the *event* that is understanding is to continue. It will serve us well, then, in avoiding misinterpretations of Gadamer's notion of understanding as a kind of unifying force that destroys all difference and movement, if we keep the notion of fusion in its proper context and conceive of it as a dynamic, interactive, ongoing activity.

SELF-TRANSFORMATION THROUGH PLAY: *ERFAHRUNG* AND *BILDUNG*

Through the play-process with the strange meaning offered by tradition, our understanding is transformed. When we break down this play-process, we recognize the key moves in which this transformation takes place. In the process of reading a traditionary text, for example, the text first addresses us with its meaning, with its claim to truth, and draws us into the hermeneutic circle. We come to the text with our own set of assumptions with which we always begin and which make up that background understanding or context of meaning in which we integrate new experiences. We take a stab at interpretation based on what we already know, and the text replies ("that's not yet what I mean"). Through our experience of the "other" meaning the text offers, which resists or denies our projected presuppositions that usually go unnoticed, our presuppositions become foregrounded in a way that makes it possible for us to examine them (their origin and validity) and alter them so that we may improve our understanding. We continue a back-and-forth process of revising our prejudgments until the meaningful whole we project is confirmed by all the details of the text. We are close, now, to grasping the claim to truth made on us; but we must, finally, answer the claim by interpreting its contemporary relevance *to us*. We only truly understand the truth articulated to us when we *apply it*, or understand it in terms of the world in which *we live*.

All of these elements that make up the play-process of understanding tradition in its various forms are, in fact, important elements of the play-process of understanding *any* new meaning we encounter. Gadamer wants us to recognize, though, that the improved understanding of the subject matter that takes place through our engaged play with new meaning is also an improved *self*-understanding. All understanding (*Verstehen*), for Gadamer, is self-understanding (*Sichverstehen*).

We saw how, in one sense, an improved self-understanding means becoming aware of our own prejudices or present horizon of understanding in a way that makes it possible for us to revise it. In this sense it means seeing ourselves, perhaps for the first time. But an improved understanding of the subject matter also means, Gadamer points out, being well versed in something: "It implies the general possibility of interpreting, of seeing connections, of drawing conclusions" (TM, 260). This means "knowing one's way around" something, and in this way implies self-understanding in a second sense—that is, as a kind of ability and comfortability with the subject matter and with one's own relationship to it

It is important to recognize that an enriched understanding and self-understanding is something that can only occur in and through our experience of some *other* meaning than our own, for this is what (1) provokes our own prejudgments into play, (2) causes us to become aware of them, and (3) allows us to revise them in such a way that we may come to "know our way around" the subject matter better. The conflict, friction, or resistance we meet in our encounter with something new, different, or *other* is a crucial aspect of what Gadamer calls genuine experience (*Erfahrung*). Gadamer declares that experience (*Erfahrung*) is a process that is essentially negative and characterized by a *disappointment* of expectations. It is a process in which "false generalizations are continually refuted" and "what was regarded as typical is shown not to be so" (TM, 353). This leads to the formation of new, better generalizations to replace the old ones. Experience in the rich and genuine sense, for Gadamer, is not that experience that simply confirms what we already think, but is the experience of something different and surprising—it is *new* experience in which our expectations are thwarted. The negativity involved in genuine experience, though, does not simply have a negative effect on us; it is positive and productive in that it is through the disappointment of our presuppositions that we become aware of the fact that our understanding has been incorrect, and have the chance to correct it or, at least, improve it. Though our experience of negativity involves a kind of pain, and is something we undergo and suffer, it is the kind of growing pain proper to development, and from it we emerge with new insight. Opening ourselves to such new, negative experience, and the difficulties proper to it— that is, opening ourselves to a back-and-forth engaged play with what is "other"—means entering a process in which we can revise what we thought we new before and, ultimately, know better.[23]

Through genuine experience, we are transformed and emerge anew with a fuller and richer understanding, which is also always richer self-understanding. This cultivated understanding and self-understanding constitutes for us a newfound *freedom* in which we feel at home in what may have previously been strange and posed a limitation to us. This cultivated understanding means that our horizon of understanding has shifted so that we are able to see beyond what limited our vision before. What was perplexing and resisted us, what we experienced as alienating and what thwarted our expectations, we have now come to understand and make our own. This transformation is exactly what learning, education, cultivation, and formation is all about. It is the process of human development we undergo that Hegel called *Bildung*. Through *Bildung* we develop beyond the nearsightedness of our own particularity—that is, beyond the immediacy of our personal feelings, desires, needs, and beyond our private interests and purposes. This "moving beyond" happens through the kind of self-restraint and work involved in opening ourselves up to other strange perspectives, and rising to more universal points of view. This *openness to and engagement with what is other*, which we already saw was crucial for the movement of play, is crucial for the movement of *Bildung*. Gadamer states early on, with regard to his notion of understanding in the human sciences and its relation to *Bildung*:

> It is not enough to observe more closely, to study a tradition more thoroughly, if there is not already a receptivity to the "otherness" of the work of art or of the past. That is what, following Hegel, we emphasized as the general characteristic of *Bildung*: keeping oneself open to what is other—to other, more universal points of view. (TM, 17)

In the notion of *Bildung* we see how, by confronting and dealing with what is alien, we are able to move from a kind of parochial understanding to one that embraces wider and richer phenomena, and grow as human beings. Gadamer notes:

> Rising to the universal is not limited to theoretical *Bildung* and does not mean only a theoretical orientation in contrast to a practical one, but covers the essential character of human rationality as a whole. . . . Whoever abandons himself to his particularity is *ungebildet* ("unformed")—e.g., if someone gives way to blind anger without measure or sense of proportion. . . . Every single individual who raises himself out of his natural being to the spiritual finds in the language, customs, and institutions of his people a pre-given body of material which, as in learning to speak, he has to make his own. Thus every individual is always engaged in the process of *Bildung* and in getting beyond his naturalness, inasmuch as the world into which he is growing is one that is humanly constituted through language and custom. (TM, 12, 14)

Rising to the universal is what Hegel takes to be the fundamental task for man. It is a process that constitutes the basic movement of spirit in which spirit journeys through self-alienation, facing what is other, toward an ultimate homecoming of full self-understanding. Whether or not we believe that this journey ever reaches an end,[24] we can see that *closing* ourselves off or disengaging from the otherness or difference which stands before us, and withdrawing from genuine play, results in a lack of learning and a stunted growth.

The movement of play is the basic movement in which we learn and develop as human beings, for it is our back-and-forth engagement with otherness in which genuine *Erfahrung* and *Bildung* occur. The comportment of openness that is necessary for such a play-engagement to occur is something that is, then, ultimately crucial for us to cultivate in ourselves. A comportment of openness to play is something that seems to be cultivated through the process of playing itself. We can see this when we consider the one who is, what we might call, "experienced" in play. Experience itself, Gadamer argues, is fundamentally always open to new experience, and inevitably the development or *Bildung* that occurs in and through experience is always open-ended. One cannot reach a point where she has experienced everything, so that no more experience can be had. On the contrary, the one who has undergone a significant amount of experience and development is actually the one who approaches new experience and development with the greatest openness. Gadamer claims: "The experienced person proves to be . . . someone who is radically undogmatic; who, because of the many experiences he has had and the knowledge he has drawn from them, is particularly well equipped to have new experiences and to learn from them" (TM, 355). Being experienced means being particularly open to new experiences out of having learned—from experience—that our knowledge is limited and always fundamentally incomplete.

Here we have uncovered a third important sense in which the enriched understanding we develop through experience is simultaneously an enriched self-understanding; for through genuine experience we come to realize in a profound way the *finitude* that characterizes who we are as human beings. Along with this realization comes an appreciation of the importance of new experiences that will allow our limited and situated horizons of understanding to shift, broaden, and become enriched. Experience teaches us that engaging in the process of play with what is "other" is the path on which our understanding and self-understanding are transformed and we truly develop as human beings.

THE PLAY OF INTERLOCUTORS: UNDERSTANDING AS DIALOGUE

In articulating the otherness or the strange meaning we experience in a work of art, a text, or any other form of tradition, Gadamer has, all along, spoken of the way different forms of tradition *speak* to us, have something to *say* to us, and *address* us. At this point, it becomes clear that this is not a mere metaphor. Tradition, Gadamer asserts, "is *language* [*Sprache*]—i.e., it expresses itself like a Thou. A Thou is not an object; it relates itself to us" (TM, 358). Our understanding of tradition is not knowledge of some object. It is not a subjective relation to some dead thing. It is, rather, a relation between I and Thou (*Ich und Du*)—a Thou who speaks to us across time and makes some claim to truth about our world, our reality. In tradition we hear the articulation of some other human being, which makes tradition, as Gadamer insists, "a genuine partner in dialogue" (TM, 358). The experience we have with the traditionary work of art or text in which we come to understand the otherness of its meaning, Gadamer explains, *is the experience of the voice of the Other* who speaks to us from the past. This is an experience whose structure is ultimately that of *dialogue* (*Gespräch*). It is with this turn to the play-process of understanding *as dialogue* that the essence of hermeneutics shines through, and Hermes himself appears.

Hermes, the ancient Greek "messenger-of-the-gods" after which hermeneutics is named, acted as a mediator between gods and mortals, announcing, translating, and communicating meaning in a form that could be grasped by both divine and human beings. The work of Hermes, on a basic level, is to make it possible for someone to understand someone else about something. Hermes brings one understanding-being's meaning, which is initially encountered as alien, obscure, or incomprehensible by another understanding-being, to comprehensibility. In doing this, two beings who were at first separated are now in meaningful, communicative contact with each other; alienation is overcome through shared understanding. Hermeneutics, in the mediating spirit of Hermes, is concerned with this same process of overcoming the alienation of meaning and bringing about a shared understanding. Just as Hermes was the famous "go-between" of the ancient world, the true locus of hermeneutics is also, as Gadamer calls it, the "in-between"—the space where the bridge that makes communication possible is to be built. The task of hermeneutics—as a theory and practice of interpretation—is to grasp how the mediating work of Hermes can be achieved, and to achieve it. The problem of hermeneutics, simply put, is the problem of how it is possible for someone to understand someone else about something.

In Gadamer's shift to describing the event of understanding in terms of a conversation or dialogue, we hear his original description of authentic participation in play echoing loudly. Just as the genuine player had to lend himself to the game and allow the game to lead him, the genuine interlocutor must allow the subject matter and its truth to be his guide. Gadamer states: "To conduct a conversation means to allow oneself to be conducted by the subject matter to which the partners in the dialogue are oriented" (TM, 367). Just as play was not a subjective act, and the game had a life of its own in which we became caught up, a dialogue too has a spirit of its own in which we become wholly involved. Gadamer states:

> We say that we "conduct" a conversation, but the more genuine a conversation is, the less its conduct lies within the will of either partner. Thus a genuine conversation is never the one that we wanted to conduct. . . . The way one word follows another, with the conversation taking its own twists and reaching its own conclusion, may well be conducted in some way, but the partners conversing are far less the leaders of it than the led. No one knows in advance what will "come out" of a conversation . . . all this shows that a conversation has a spirit of its own, and that the language in which it is conducted bears its own truth within it—i.e., that it allows something to "emerge" which henceforth exists. (TM, 383)

To engage in a dialogue in which a joint understanding of truth is sought, is to participate in the movement of play with the Other and become caught up in the game of the subject matter itself and its unfolding truth.

The game of understanding—a game that is bigger than our individual roles in it, a game to which we as players belong and lend ourselves, and a game through which truth emerges—is ultimately shown by Gadamer to be the game of language. Our play with the Other is a linguistic play in which I and Thou jointly aim to articulate or give an account of some truth about our shared world. The "fusion of horizons," which occurs in this joint achievement of understanding, "*is the achievement of language*" (TM, 378). When we are trying to come to an understanding of the subject matter with one another—whether through the medium of a text, any other form of tradition, or face to face—"what emerges in its truth is the logos, which is neither mine nor yours and hence so far transcends the interlocutors' subjective opinions that even the person leading the conversation knows that he does not know" (TM, 368). Language is not a private possession or tool, but is something shared, and (as we saw with tradition) is something that precedes us and we inherit, but which we also appropriate and develop anew. In the dialogue in which truth and understanding emerge, I and Thou both begin with the language they have inherited, and aim to create a common language that can articulate the truth of the subject matter under discussion. Gadamer states:

> Hence reaching an understanding on the subject-matter of a conversation necessarily means that a common language must first be worked out in the conversation. This is not an external matter of simply adjusting our tools; nor is it even right to say that the partners adapt themselves to one another but, rather, in a successful conversation they both come under the influence of the truth of the object and are thus bound to one another in a new community. To

reach an understanding in a dialogue is not merely a matter of putting oneself forward and successfully asserting one's own point of view, but being transformed into a communion in which we do not remain what we were. (TM, 379)

This is the communion of a game in which we participate with others in dialogue—a language game in which the truth of the subject matter finds its articulation and, through our voices, presents itself.

Bringing this fundamental insight into view opens up for us a horizon in which we can turn to focus more closely on the ethical dimensions of understanding; for now we can see that the play-process of our hermeneutical experience is a play between I and Thou. Understanding itself is a dialogical event that relies, as we will see, upon a particular kind of I-Thou relation in order to occur.

NOTES

1. Gadamer is not the first to expand the domain of hermeneutics. He recognizes Wilhelm Dilthey for his efforts to extend hermeneutics beyond its original domain of theology and philology, and to ground the human sciences as a whole in hermeneutics; but he is also critical of Dilthey's understanding of hermeneutics in terms of historical consciousness.

2. Heidegger's discussion of the hermeneutic circle is meant to account for the structure of *Dasein*'s (the human being's) understanding as his very mode of being-in-the-world. The circle for Heidegger is, thus, ontological. Gadamer, along with Heidegger, believes that understanding is *Dasein*'s mode of being, and so it is also ontological for Gadamer. But here he uses it to describe the understanding of history in the human sciences.

3. Gadamer appropriates the concept of "horizon" from Husserl. He states that with the concept Husserl sought to "capture the way all limited intentionality of meaning merges into the fundamental continuity of the whole" (TM, 245). Gadamer, similarly, uses the concept to capture the way our past and present understanding and self-understanding meld together in a continuous manner, and to show the way in which we can only grasp new experiences by integrating them into our present context of meaning. This process of integration, in turn, transforms and alters that context, allowing it to shift and move, even grow and become enriched. The fact that human life is always involved in historical movement means that we are never bound to any one standpoint, but that our standpoint is always shifting. Likewise, the context of meaning or horizon of understanding that surrounds us is also always shifting. As we move so does our horizon. Seeing a new and different point of view as true is a way of broadening our horizon, gaining a higher vantage point, or more universal point of view.

4. With this insight, Gadamer is able to defend himself against the criticism characteristic of one of his most influential critics, Jürgen Habermas, who claims that giving prejudices a positive role in understanding makes understanding itself subservient to the (oppressive) authority of tradition. Habermas, contra Gadamer, wishes to preserve the Enlightenment distinction between tradition and reason and looks to reason to help emancipate us from the power imbalances propagated in tradition. He believes that there is a kind of "reflection," as he puts it in his "Review of *Truth and Method*," that is not bound to the claims of tradition and is, thus, able to reject them outright. Reflection can, thus, "shake the dogmatism" of tradition (Jürgen Habermas, "Review of *Truth and Method*" in *The Hermeneutic Tradition: From Ast to Ricoeur*, ed.

Gayle L. Ormiston and Alan D. Schrift [Albany: SUNY Press, 1990], 236–37). This is a major point of contention in the so-called Gadamer-Habermas debate. Habermas feels that by legitimating the influence of tradition and prejudices on our thinking as a condition for the possibility of any knowledge at all, Gadamer is in effect denying us the possibility of any sort of genuine critique or break from tradition in which we might overcome the different forms of oppression handed down through it. For this reason he calls Gadamer a conservative. According to Gadamer, there is room in his hermeneutics for critique, which is an integral part of the appropriation of tradition in which we make it our own; but, he believes, we are fooling ourselves if we think we can somehow reason, reflect, or criticize from outside the tradition in which we always exist as historically situated beings, and which always influences our thinking in some way.

5. Here legal and theological hermeneutics serve as exemplars of this truth. It is only in the application of a law—either of the state or of God—to a concrete situation that it is understood. Discovering the law's meaning and how to apply it are both parts of the same process of understanding. The normative and cognitive functions of understanding cannot be separated. We will return to the significance of application in understanding in chapter 7.

6. The hermeneutical task that is set for us to accomplish if we are going to understand a work of art, text, or other form of tradition is, as Gadamer has emphasized, historical mediation in which the gulf between our present and the meaning calling out from the past is overcome. From these remarks on the necessity of *application* for such a mediation to be achieved, we can see that "reconstruction" cannot be the proper way of defining the hermeneutical task, as Schleiermacher had thought. An attempt to reconstruct the original context of the work and the state of mind of the author is not only futile (considering that we are historically situated beings who cannot live in the past), but also would not produce for us the living relationship with the traditionary work necessary for it to become meaningful. *Resuscitating* dead meaning *through historical mediation* means engaging it in a way that makes it meaningful *for us*, integrating it into *our lives* and, thus, bringing it back to life. "[A] hermeneutics that regarded understanding as reconstructing the original would be no more than handing on a dead meaning" (TM, 167).

7. Chapter 5 will look closer at the ethical dimension of this problem.

8. Jürgen Habermas, "Review of *Truth and Method*," in *The Hermeneutic Tradition*, ed. *The Hermeneutic Tradition: From Ast to Ricoeur*, ed. Gayle L. Ormiston and Alan D. Schrift (Albany: SUNY Press, 1990).

9. Habermas, "Review," 236.

10. Habermas, "Review," 236.

11. Habermas, "Review," 236.

12. Habermas, "Review," 237.

13. Jürgen Habermas, "Knowledge and Human Interests," in *Knowledge and Human Interests*, trans. Jeremy Shapiro (Boston: Beacon Press, 1971).

14. Habermas, "Knowledge," 310.

15. Habermas, "Knowledge," 310.

16. Habermas, "Review," 238.

17. Emilio Betti, "Hermeneutics as the General Methodology of the *Geisteswissenschaften*," in *Contemporary Hermeneutics* by Josef Bleicher (London and New York: Routledge & Kegan Paul, 1980).

18. Betti, "General Methodology," 76.

19. We see a similar concern voiced by another early critic of Gadamer, E. D. Hirsch, who in his *Validity in Interpretation* argues, with regard to Gadamer's notion of understanding: "If the interpreter is really bound by his own historicity, he cannot break out of it into some halfway house where past and present are merged. At best he can only gather up the leftover, unspeaking inscriptions from the past and wring from them, or impose on them, some meaning in terms of his own historical perspective." E. D. Hirsch, *Validity in Interpretation* (New Haven and London: Yale University Press, 1967), 254. Hirsch, here, is also worried that Gadamer's notion of understanding as a

fusion of horizons ultimately amounts to the projection of the interpreter's own meaning onto the text.

20. Betti, "General Methodology," 79.

21. Betti, "General Methodology," 80.

22. An example of one of these critics is Robert Bernasconi, who argues that "the notion of the fusion of horizons seems fundamentally antagonistic to alterity" in "You Don't Know What I'm Talking About: Alterity and the Hermeneutical Ideal," in *The Specter of Relativism,* ed. Lawrence Schmidt (Evanston, Ill.: Northwestern University Press, 1995), 187.

23. This kind of experience Gadamer calls, following Hegel, dialectical. But, as we will see in chapter 6, the insight that negativity can be productive takes us all the way back to Socrates' famous practice of *elenchus*.

24. Whereas Hegel believes there is a final absolutizing moment when spirit finally comes to know itself completely, Gadamer believes that the process of understanding and self-understanding, and of *Bildung*, is an open-ended one. Gadamer recognizes his deep indebtedness to Hegel, but disagrees with him on this major point. For Gadamer, the fact of our human finitude will not allow the achievement of a final and complete knowledge and self-knowledge. According to him, we are instead *always on the way* along a journey that will never reach a final destination.

Part III

The Ethical Dimensions of Play

Chapter 5

The Ethical Conditions of Dialogic Play: Between I and Thou

Having set out in *Truth and Method* to correct false thinking about what happens to us when understanding takes place, and to illuminate the real experience that understanding in general is, Gadamer first turned to the experience of a work of art. In the encounter with a work of art, Gadamer found artwork and spectator to be interactive partners in a back-and-forth play-movement that absorbs the players in its unique rhythm and takes on a life of its own. We saw in this discussion that it is *only in and through* the engagement of play that meaning emerges, the artwork finds its completion, and understanding is achieved. We went on to discover that play is not only the process of our interpretive experience of watching a stage performance, hearing a song, or viewing a painting; it is through the same process that we read, interpret, and understand texts of all kinds. This led us to a perspective in which we could see play as the process by which our hermeneutic experiences of tradition in any of its forms— "whether art or the other spiritual creations of the past: law, religion, philosophy, and so forth"—take place (TM, 165). In fact, we came to see play as the process of all of our hermeneutic experiences in which we grasp meaning. The play-process of understanding finally revealed itself to be a process of communication that occurs between I and Thou. Thus, the back-and-forth movement that we found to be the driving force of *all* hermeneutic experience finally emerged as *dialogic* play.

When the play-process of understanding is finally recognized to have the fundamental form of *dialogue*, the first of the distinctly ethical dimensions of play—and the understanding that emerges in and through it— comes to the fore in a more explicit way. It now becomes apparent that the dynamic event of play in which understanding occurs relies on a particular kind of relation between I and Thou. Hermeneutic experience is not the experience of some object, but of the articulation of some other human being. It is the experience of what some "Other" says to us in language.[1] Gadamer argues that the tradition that we come to understand in the human sciences (or as a basic part of our inheritance and upbringing) "expresses itself like a Thou" and is therefore a "genuine partner in dialogue" (*Kommunikationspartner*) (TM, 358; WM, 364). Since our experience of tradition is an experience in which we interact with some "Thou" who speaks to us, it is a "moral phenomenon" (TM, 358). Now, it is true that the Thou who articulates something to us in and through tradition may not address us "in the flesh" or "face-to-face." In fact, this Thou may no longer exist as a living, breathing Thou at all. His meaningful articulation and his claim to truth that we encounter — if we encounter it through a work of art or text, for instance — is detached from his living breath and has acquired a life of its own in the world. But, nevertheless, the way in which we engage this Thou's claim to truth, through his or her work of art or text, and come to understand what is said to us across time, follows the model of a living dialogue in crucial ways. Examining the kind of relationship we have with the Thou in living dialogue, when a shared understanding about some subject matter takes place, will teach us how we come to an understanding in our hermeneutical experience in general.

So, what kind of relationship between I and Thou is necessary for a common understanding of some subject matter to come about? Or, in other words, what kind of interaction between I and Thou creates the kind of dialogue in which a shared understanding develops? And what does it take for us to achieve this kind of dialogue? In order to highlight the answer, we will consider three models or types of I-Thou relations that Gadamer describes. I will refer to them as (A) a scientific approach to the Other, (B) a psychological approach to the Other, and (C) an "open" approach to the Other. By considering first the two I-Thou relations in which Gadamer finds a failure to achieve real dialogue and understanding, we will be able to better appreciate the distinctiveness of Gadamer's third, "highest" type of I-Thou relation, where we find a unique approach and commitment to the Other that makes genuine dialogic play and true understanding possible. It is in this third I-Thou relation that we find the "ethical conditions" of dialogic play present, which make it possible for a shared understanding to develop. These conditions I call "ethical" because (1) they are the manner in which human interlocutors *must treat each other* for dialogic play to continue and flourish; (2) these I-Thou relations create an encounter with the Other that is characterized by mutual *respect* (i.e., treating the Other like a human being who has something meaningful to say, rather than an object to be dominated); (3) these I-Thou relations require a shared *commitment* and self-disciplined *conduct* to be achieved; and (4) these I-Thou relations ultimately provide for a process in which mutual human growth can occur, making them I-Thou relations that are ultimately *directed toward our common human good.*

FOUL PLAY: A SCIENTIFIC APPROACH TO THE OTHER

First, Gadamer tells us, "There is a kind of experience of the Thou that tries to discover typical behavior in one's fellowmen and can make predictions about others on the basis of experience" (TM, 358). In this type of experience, the Thou is approached as a natural object to be observed and examined. The examining "I" who approaches the Thou as a "thing" stands at a distance from his object (on guard against being influenced by its behavior) so that it may objectively categorize its qualities, calculate its movements, and discover the "truth" harbored inside the thing—that is, its "nature." The knowledge that the "I" acquires through his study of the Other-as-thing is meant to enable him to anticipate the thing's future behavior and develop some sort of control, mastery, or dominance over it. This particular manner of approaching another human being and trying to understand him—an approach characterized by distance, objectification, and dominance—is, in short, that of the natural scientist. In this case the I-Thou relation is reduced to an I-It relation.

We can see almost immediately how this approach to the Other impedes the sort of dialogical play-process that would allow a higher, mutual understanding to develop. Approaching the Other as a thing, rather than a person who has something significant to say from which one might learn, means immediately closing one's ears to the "claim to truth" of the Other. A patient might experience this sort of approach to the Other at a doctor's examination if the doctor, for instance, does only physical tests, talking with the patient only insofar as he can get answers to factual questions like "does this hurt?" In this scenario, the doctor neither asks about nor listens to the patient's own knowledge of the history of his illness and the past failed attempts at solving it. The doctor may even leave the room before offering his diagnosis (interpretation) of the problem, or explaining his reasons for prescribing the drug or course of therapy that he hands off to the nurse to administer. In this case the patient experiences being an object of study that is passively undergoing a procedure of observation, but he experiences no real dialogue in which knowledge is shared and a higher understanding is reached. In this case neither the patient nor the doctor learns what the other can contribute to a greater understanding of the specific ailment at hand, since no dialogue about this subject matter is undertaken.

A second important problem with the scientific approach to the Other is entangled with the first problem mentioned. The scientific approach to the Other not only fails to achieve the goal of a higher understanding of some subject matter, it actually involves a fundamental attitude of disrespect toward the Other. Treating the Other as an object, instead of a human being who has something of value to say, means disregarding (in Kantian language) the "dignity" of the Other and ignoring his humanity. Gadamer explains: "From the moral point of view this orientation toward the Thou is purely self-regarding and contradicts the moral definition of man. As we know, in interpreting the categorical imperative Kant said, inter alia, that the other should never be used as a means but always as an end in himself" (TM, 358).[2] When we treat the Other as an object (as a means to our own end, or a being with only instrumental value) and not as a subject (as an end in himself, or a being with absolute value) we take on a posture of dominance that severs the basic moral relation that is needed if we are to enter into a meaningful dialogue with the Other about some subject matter and reach a shared understanding about it. This basic moral relation is the relation of a subject to a subject, in which there is a reciprocal recognition of each other's full humanity. (In the above example, the doctor's "objectifying" approach to the patient is likely to be offensive enough to the patient that it will make him switch doctors.)

When we confront the Other who speaks to us, either face to face or through tradition, as an object, we ignore the voice of the Other and the Other's meaningful articulation. In doing so, we not only halt the potential for dialogue, we also ignore the real humanity of the Thou who speaks to us. We turn our backs, close our ears, and deny him the kind of recognition that is involved in listening to his claim to truth. We remove ourselves from a relationship with the Other in which we might be affected, learn something, and be transformed. When we treat the Other like an object, we allow him merely to make sounds, but not to speak meaningfully. In this case, there can be no dialogue in which we might share an understanding with the Other.

FOUL PLAY: A PSYCHOLOGICAL APPROACH TO THE OTHER

"A second way in which the Thou is experienced and understood is that the Thou is acknowledged as a person, but despite this acknowledgment the understanding of the Thou is still a form of self-relatedness" (TM, 359). What Gadamer is getting at here is that in the psychological approach to the Other, the Other is still treated as a kind of "thing," but in this case he is treated as a "psychological thing." In this I-Thou relation one hears what the Other says as a meaningful statement—even as a unique enunciation of meaning *other* than one's own—but one takes the Other's statement to be the expression of his personal attitude, an expression of his life (*Lebensäußerung*), or of his life experience (*Erlebnis*), and attempts to understand it only as his (idiosyncratic) point of view. The "I" in this scenario understands what the "Thou" expresses in strictly psychological terms. The "I" even claims to know the "Thou," through a psychological-biographical study, better than the Thou knows himself.

Even though we find a step of improvement in this second I-Thou relation, since the "I" now (at least) listens to what the Other has to say, there is still a problem with the *way* that the "I" listens. The "I" in this scenario does not listen to what the other has to say as a "claim to truth," but as a reflection of the other's "self." The "I" does not recognize the "Thou" as a being that has something meaningful to say about *the way the world is*, about *the truth* of things, but only as a being that is capable of expressing the way he "feels," or the way he sees things as a result of his personal life history. Gadamer explains: "By understanding the other, by claiming to know him, one robs his claims of their legitimacy. . . . The claim to understand the other person in advance functions to keep the other person's claim at a distance" (TM, 360). The problem, in short, is that the "I," here, does not take what the "Thou" says seriously. Taking the Other seriously would mean treating what he has to say as a potential *truth* that could transform the way we think and act, rather than as a mere attitude, a subjective reflection, or a product of some life event which colors all of his thoughts. Not taking what the Other says seriously, and seeing all of his thoughts as psychological constructs, rather than as truth claims, not only blocks the possibility of a mutually transforming dialogue about some subject matter in which a common understanding might occur, but also simultaneously disrespects the Other with whom one is speaking. Again, we have a problem of the Thou being treated not as a full human being who has something to contribute to a shared understanding of our world, but as a peculiar kind of thing.

We can easily recognize when someone is approaching us as a "psychological thing." The minute the pop-psychoanalyst we meet at a dinner party discovers some fact about our childhood, our financial situation, our political party, our religion, the state in which we were born, and so on, he believes he knows everything else we might possibly think or say. As soon as we try to make some point about the "truth" of the issue under discussion, our pop-psychoanalyst will interpret what we say in terms of an apparently determining factoid from our past. I say: "I think we need to recognize that human beings are not the only ones who inhabit this earth. Our actions are negatively affecting all the other forms of life on this planet." He says: "Aren't you from the West Coast? Ah, I bet you were taught to feel guilty about throwing away a soda can in primary school." In this case one can't help but know that one is not being taken seriously and that any real dialogue about the subject matter will not get underway until one is.

Insofar as the Other in this second I-Thou relation is taken to be another human being who is capable of interpreting his experiences and talking about them, this I-Thou relation is more moral than the one that treats the Other as a natural object. Unlike the scientific I-Thou relation above, this psychological I-Thou relation can involve a kind of reciprocity where both I and Thou try to understand each other; but this is done in a way where there is a struggle to "outdo" each other, or where both claim to know the Other better than the Other knows himself. It is still, then, a relationship in which mastery, control, and dominance is attempted over the Other, and the Other is thus devalued, belittled, and disrespected. The psychological approach to the Other (like the scientific approach to the Other) is characterized by a kind of distance in which the "I" remains removed from a real engagement with the "Thou" due to the "I's" unwillingness to recognize the Thou's truth claims and allow himself to be affected, transformed, or educated in his encounter with the "Thou." Any sort of mutually transforming dialogue or improved understanding about some common subject matter, therefore, still cannot get started.

It is important to pause here a moment with regard to this second I-Thou relation, because its description recalls Gadamer's analysis and critique of Schleiermacher's conception of understanding (which ulti-mately finds its expression as "historical consciousness" via Dilthey). The psychological approach to the Other has become, because of Schleier-macher and Dilthey, highly influential as a method for interpretation in the human sciences and, thus, constitutes a much more serious and far-reaching hermeneutic model than my example of the pop-psychoanalyst above suggests. This psychological model of interpretation is so influen-tial that it is the model that most first-time students of Gadamer anticipate the process of "understanding each other" must follow. Students express this prejudgment when they declare that to understand a text, one will have to go back to the intentions of the author and do biographical research to understand what the author was thinking, what he believed, and how he felt. Though they don't know it, these students are operating on the Schleiermacherian model of understanding.

According to Schleiermacher, if we are to understand what the Other says, we must understand the individuality of the Other. The Other's words are taken by Schleiermacher to be an expression of their author's particular life, thought, and intention. For Schleiermacher, written and oral utterances are the free expression of the unique individual who utters them. They are the bursting forth of life moments, which contain an overflowing pleasure, into verbal expression and, as such, are the free creation or the aesthetic construct of the author. They are, simply put, the artistic expression of the author's life. To understand the author, we have to go back to the origin of his words. This "going back" means trying to get inside the author's mind, trying to think as he thought, and—somehow—intuit his intention. The ability to understand the author's linguistic expression and get into his shoes, or more properly his *mind* or his *life*, is thought possible by Schleiermacher because each of us, as unique individuals, have something in common with every other individ-ual by virtue of our shared humanity. Even though the other individual is fundamentally different from me in his particularity, and is in this sense an alien being, there is also something about him that is familiar. He lives a human life just like me. It is, thus, through a sympathetic feeling (TM, 191) that one comes to understand the author's meaning or hidden intention expressed in his words. In coming to know the author's life and mind, in deciphering the inner meaning, root, and origin of his expressions of which he himself is unaware, and in exposing this meaning in a way that makes conscious what was to him unconscious, one comes to know the author better than he knows himself.

In analyzing the Schleiermacherian model of understanding, Gadamer argues that Schleiermacher conceives of language merely as an "expressive field"—expressive of the author's personal life, experience, and perspective. This is a major point of contention for Gadamer, who urges us to ask: Is language really just the expression of one's personal life and feeling? Is there no knowledge to be gained by listening to another speak, or reading another's words, beyond the grasp of the author's attitude? Is there no truth to be communicated in language? Gadamer insists that linguistic statements are not "free expressions" but are articulations of some *subject matter* and make a claim to *truth*. Therefore, what we want to understand, when we try to understand another's words, is not the other person, not *who* he is, but *what* he says, or *what* meaning he presents with his words. What we want to learn, according to Gadamer, when we listen to what the Other says, is not the Other's psychological point of view, but the substantial *content* that he articulates. What we want to share with the other person when we understand him is not his idiosyncratic attitude, but *truth*. To clarify the true goals of understanding, Gadamer states:

> We begin with this proposition: "to understand means to come to an understanding with each other" (*sich miteinander verstehen*). Understanding is, primarily, agreement (*Verständnis ist zunächst Einverständnis*). Thus people usually understand (*verstehen*) each other immediately, or they make themselves understood (*verständigen sich*) with a view toward reaching agreement (*Einverständnis*). Coming to an understanding (*Verständigung*), then, is always coming to an understanding about something. Understanding each other (*sich verstehen*) is always understanding each other with respect to something. From language we learn that the subject matter (*Sache*) is not merely an arbitrary object of discussion, independent of the process of mutual understanding (*Sichverstehen*), but rather is the path and goal of mutual understanding itself. (TM, 180)

Because language for Schleiermacher is not taken to be the articulation of some subject matter, but a free expression, language for Schleiermacher lacks the ontological valence it has for Gadamer. Language for Schleiermacher is not a "bringing forth of being," as it is for Gadamer. Any "claim to truth" that might be made in language is, from Gadamer's point of view, ignored under Schleiermacher's model. Gadamer argues that taking another's utterances as mere self-expressions means that dialogue becomes, not the joint search for the truth of the subject matter, but the mutual stimulation of individual thought that gradually becomes exhausted. This is not the sort of dialogue in which a shared understanding about our world can develop. It is for Gadamer, therefore, not a genuine dialogue. Gadamer summarizes the problem he sees with the psychological approach to the other (in both the scenario of face-to-face dialogue and our attempt to understand what the other says in a historical text) in the following way:

> In a conversation, when we have discovered the other person's standpoint and horizon, his ideas become intelligible without our necessarily having to agree with him; so also when someone thinks historically, he comes to understand the meaning of what has been handed down without necessarily seeing himself in it. In both cases the person understanding has, as it were, stopped trying to reach an agreement. He himself cannot be reached. By factoring the other person's standpoint into what he is claiming to say, we are making our own standpoint safely unattainable. . . . The text that is understood historically is forced to abandon its claim to saying something true. We think we understand when we see the past from a historical standpoint—i.e., transpose ourselves into the historical situation and try to reconstruct the historical horizon. In fact, however, we have given up the claim to find in the past any truth that is valid and intelligible for ourselves. Acknowledging the otherness of the other in this way, making him the object of objective knowledge, involves the fundamental suspension of his claim to truth. (TM, 303)

Gadamer is reminding us here of what we really do when we try to understand what another says as just an expression of their personal, idiosyncratic standpoint. In this I-Thou relation, where we "suspend" the Other's claim to truth, we close ourselves off from the Other, not allowing what he says to affect us or transform our thinking. In this scenario, the "I" takes himself to be the "knower" while the Thou is the "known." What the Thou knows himself, and what might be learned from him, is ignored. A relationship of mutual understanding, teaching, and learning is neither recognized, nor achieved. Gadamer argues: "A person who reflects himself out of the mutuality of such a relation changes this relationship and destroys its moral bond. *A person who reflects himself out of a living relationship to tradition destroys the true meaning of this tradition in exactly the same way*" (TM, 360). Though we may seem to know the one speaking to us in this I-Thou relation is a human being, the full extent of his humanity is not recognized, for the Other is here treated not as one who understands something about the world that can profoundly affect our own thinking, but is, rather, treated as someone who simply has personal attitudes and a point of view built up out of private life-experiences (*Erlebnisse*). This second, psychological type of I-Thou relationship, in the end, reveals itself to be derivative of the first, for the objectification involved in the scientific approach to the other is here preserved—this time in treating the Thou as a psychological thing whose expressions are to be deciphered.

GENUINE PLAY: OPENNESS TO THE OTHER

A third and highest type of I-Thou relationship, according to Gadamer, is characterized by a comportment of "openness to the Other" (*Offenheit für den anderen*). Approaching the Other with "openness" means approaching the Other with a *readiness* to hear something meaningful and something *different* from what we already think, know, or have heard others say. But, more important, it means approaching the Other with a readiness for the Other to teach us something new—something *true*—about our world and ourselves and, thus, affect our way of thinking in a meaningful way. Whereas we saw an attempt to "master" the Other in the scientific and psychological approaches, we see here finally a *willingness to allow the Other to challenge our own preconceptions*. We have in this third I-Thou relation, finally, the kind of recognition of the Other, and what he says, that grants him equal footing as our interlocutor and partner in the play-process of articulating truth.[3] Gadamer states:

> In human relations the important thing is, as we have seen, to experience the Thou truly as a Thou—i.e., not to overlook his claim but to let him really say something to us. Here is where openness belongs. But ultimately this openness does not exist only for the person who speaks; rather, anyone who listens is fundamentally open. Without such openness to one another there is no genuine human bond. (TM, 361)

We have already seen that the "comportment of openness" is crucial for the process of understanding. All along, in Gadamer's explication of what makes understanding possible, the comportment of openness has been an essential condition for the possibility of the back-and-forth movement in which we let new meaning speak to us (through an artwork, text, or other form of tradition), in which we test and revise our prejudices, and in which we enrich our grasp of the world. We emphasized, in our discussion of the play-process of understanding in chapters 3 and 4, how much of a "commitment" is involved in this openness, and how much of a self-disciplined conduct is required to let new meaning really speak to us if we are to achieve a shared understanding. Now we are able to see more clearly the ethical nature of this commitment: it is a commitment to another human being.

We had our first glimpses of this "commitment" in Gadamer's description of the kind of play that is distinctively human, which we discussed in chapter 2. There we saw that what is peculiar about human play is that the player involves himself in a game by "wanting" and "choosing" to play and, more specifically, by restricting himself to *performing the tasks* proper to the game. Human *willingness*, we saw, is essential to the kinds of games we humans play, and the human game of understanding is no different. Our *willingness to engage the voice of the Other*, to listen and to speak, is a crucial condition of understanding. In the specific play that occurs in the experience of a work of art, we saw that the kind of committed conduct or *task* that the genuine spectator has to fulfill is to *participate* with the artwork by allowing the work to address him. In order to understand the artwork's meaning, the spectator has to lend himself to the story it aims to tell so that it can reach full presentation. This leads to the *achievement* of a mediation between past and present that allows understanding to occur. Even in the early discussion of art we saw that it is an *accomplishment* to open oneself to the voice of the Other who presents meaning to us. Accomplishing this openness requires the *work* of attending to the subject matter presented by the Other with focused determination.

Finally, in Gadamer's discussion of the play-process of understanding historical tradition, which we discussed in chapter 4, we saw that the tasks involved in mediating past and present include "appropriation" and "application" in which the interpreter has the job of relating the meaning he encounters through the voice of the Other to his own life, so that it can find its significance for him and live again for the present. This too requires an openness to the meaning spoken by the Other, and a willingness to let it affect him. Most important, in Gadamer's discussion of tradition, we saw that the tasks of understanding always involve *risking* our own prejudices, or "bringing them into play" so that they can be revised. As Gadamer put it: "Our own prejudice is properly brought into play by being put at risk. Only by being given full play is it able to experience the other's claim to truth and make it possible for him to have full play himself" (TM, 299). This task of risking our own prejudices, and of making our own understanding questionable, generates an openness toward the Other in dialogue (whether we are dialoguing with the voice of the Other through an artwork, text, or face to face) that carries with it a real recognition of the Other's full humanity. Openness means treating the Other as a being who understands, who has a different range of experiences from our own, and who can present, articulate, and share with us his view of the world in language. It is only through our openness to the Other that the Other is given "full play" —full participation in our joint articulation of truth.

It is this willingness to put oneself at risk that really distinguishes "openness to the Other" from the other I-Thou relations. In no other I-Thou relation does the "I" put himself in a position so that what he already believes may be touched, altered, even pierced through by the Other. Because of this, the "I" of the first two I-Thou relations remains always "closed" to the Other. "Risking" oneself in dialogue with the Other—putting oneself, one's beliefs, one's worldview on the line—is what allows for the Other's claim to be given its full weight, for the Other to be given his full recognition, and for the "I" to learn something new and grow in the process.

The crucial condition of "openness" for the play-process of understanding, we see now, is not only a kind of committed conduct that requires self-disciplined "work on ourselves" to achieve (as with any sort of virtue of character). It is also a conduct that governs the way we must treat the Other. "Openness" in our dialogue with the Other means treating the Other with respect—namely, as a human being and not a thing. Openness toward the other creates, in Gadamer's view, an authentic encounter with the Other that allows for the possibility of greater mutual understanding which, for Gadamer (as we cannot ignore and will consider more closely in chapter 7), is ultimately *good for us*! The comportment of openness, thus, reveals itself to be a crucial ethical condition for genuine dialogue and understanding.

OPENNESS AND THE AWARENESS OF HUMAN FINITUDE

Essential to the *openness* to the Other and the meaningful *content* of what the Other says, Gadamer explains, is the recognition that our own knowledge is always situated and incomplete and that we can learn something from our engagement with other human beings. In other words, the stance of openness means that we are able to recognize that our own horizon of understanding is limited by our own historical situation. It means we are aware of our "historically effected consciousness" (*wirkungsgeschichtliche Bewußtsein*).[4] The recognition of the situatedness of our own understanding, and the limitations it involves, implies an undogmatic attitude and an awareness that we can't know everything, that our current understanding is probably rather flawed about many things, and that we can always learn something new or expand our understanding through our engagements with others in which our old ideas are challenged. "Openness to the other, then, involves recognizing that I myself must accept some things that are against me, even though no one else forces me to do so" (TM, 361). An openness toward history means the same thing, for as Gadamer states, "I must allow tradition's claim to validity not in the sense of simply acknowledging the past in its otherness, but in such a way that it has something to say to me. This too calls for a fundamental sort of openness" (TM, 361). A recognition of our own hermeneutical situation and, thus, our own finitude means that we understand not only our limitations, but also what our possibilities for growth are. The undogmatic one who is open to the Other acknowledges that, even though understanding is historically situated, we are not held captive by our prejudices; we are, in fact, able to have new experiences and new dialogues with others, which allow our horizons of meaning to shift and open up. In fact, there are many truths about our world that, as Gadamer puts it, "becom[e] visible to me only through the Thou, and only by my letting myself be told something by it" (TM, xxxv). We need not worry that "being situated" implies that a person is locked into a parochial view of things, or that his horizon is closed. A person's horizon is something that moves with him as he moves through time and encounters new things and people. A horizon, thus, is fundamentally open to change. As we move in the back-and-forth dialogic play with other human beings, our horizons shift and even find new spaces of overlap with the horizons of meaning of individuals whose situations are quite different from our own. This is another way of understanding what Gadamer means by the fusion of horizons that occurs in understanding. It is not just a fusion of horizons between past and present, but it is a fusion of horizons between I and Thou in dialogue—and for Gadamer such a fusion, though it may take considerable effort, time, and commitment, is always in principle possible.[5] The stance of openness to the Other, through which we might achieve such a fusion of horizons, coincides with an understanding of our own nature as historically finite, fundamentally open to new experiences, and fundamentally open to enriching our understanding through our encounters with others. The open approach to dialogue and the awareness of our own finitude constitute two sides of the same coin of what Gadamer calls "hermeneutic consciousness."

PRESERVING THE OTHERNESS OF THE OTHER

At this point we must return again to our discussion of Gadamer's critics and their worries regarding his notion of understanding as a fusion of horizons. Earlier we considered the fusion of horizons in its "vertical sense," referring to the fusion between past and present that takes place when we understand the meaning handed down by tradition. Now, when we consider the fusion of horizons in its "horizontal sense," referring to the fusion that takes place when understanding occurs between different peoples, or between I and Thou in living dialogue, the ethical dimension of the charges made against Gadamer come to light more fully.[6] Let us consider again the charge that Gadamer's notion of understanding as a fusion of horizons is fundamentally antagonistic to alterity, otherness, and difference. When this fusion is one between I and Thou, the charge becomes that understanding is a project that results in ignoring, excluding, and diminishing the otherness of the Other. If understanding aims only at overcoming alienation, then it views difference merely as a *problem* to reconcile. It aims to constantly homogenize the variety of human viewpoints and smooth over the tension between them.[7] This is taken by many of Gadamer's critics to be not only an impossible task, because they believe that there is an irreducible plurality of human experiences and standpoints, but also to be a project that is ethically suspect—for it means fundamentally denying the Other any genuine recognition of his real difference and individuality and suppressing diversity.

Robert Bernasconi, in his article "'You Don't Know What I'm Talking About': Alterity and the Hermeneutic Ideal," suggests that, when faced with a situation in which Gadamer's interlocutor tells him "You don't know what I'm talking about" and in effect denies that understanding is possible between them, Gadamer "would still be committed to anticipating an agreement that is being refused."[8] Bernasconi claims that Gadamer's notion of understanding is fundamentally directed toward "agreement," and is therefore a process in which the difference of the Other is ultimately assimilated by the interpreter. In his conclusion, Bernasconi considers a question Gadamer once asked of himself about how far he had succeeded in "preserving and not simply assimilating the Otherness of the Other in understanding." Bernasconi's answer to this question is that Gadamer had not sufficiently succeeded in doing so in the theory he had laid out in *Truth and Method*. He argues that Gadamer does not sufficiently recognize the claim of the Other who insists: "You don't know what I'm talking about," explaining:

> The phrase says, "You cannot be yourself and understand me." It not only says "this is you": it also implies "you ought to change," and yet at the same time acknowledges that the change won't—in a sense, can't—take place. Women say it to men; the poor say it to the rich; the victim says it to the oppressor; the target of racism says it to the racist.[9]

This is a claim that refuses the possibility of understanding, and declares—*as the truth*—that understanding is impossible between us. Gadamer, according to Bernasconi, is unable to recognize the real difference being claimed here by the Other because Gadamer already treats the Other as someone with whom he has a bond in sharing a language, tradition, or world with him. In other words, within the Gadamerian picture of understanding, the "One" always approaches the "Other" from the start as "his" Other. Gadamer's understanding, according to Bernasconi, amounts to the One making his Other so much his own that he comes to see himself in his Other. In this case Bernasconi believes that Gadamer is not sufficiently recognizing what genuine difference really means— namely, that it is something that cannot simply be grasped by another and joined together with another's understanding into a continuous whole. According to Bernasconi, what Gadamer does not grasp is that

> misunderstanding is not a contingent phenomenon that occasionally threatens the possibility of genuine understanding and can be corrected. That "you don't know what I'm talking about" reveals a more fundamental sense of misunderstanding, the misunderstanding that pervades all understanding and that compromises the Gadamerian picture.[10]

The philosophical underpinning of these comments, I take it, is that real individuality is something that is so singular and unique that it, and its expressions, simply cannot be fully grasped by others. If we would take individuality seriously, we would recognize that there are gaps, fissures, and abysses between us that can never be fully bridged. To ignore this fact, and to continually believe that one has or can come to a full understanding with others in conversation, is to disrespect the uniqueness that is fundamental to human individuality.

This is a criticism that receives its philosophical inspiration from the work of Derrida, who above all wants to uncover and preserve difference and plurality, and to reveal the cracks that always penetrate what we take to be whole, the breaks that cannot be fused—the two inside the one. While Derrida thinks, writes, and speaks from a basic sensibility that human existence is characterized by all sorts of unbridgeable gaps, Gadamer operates with the basic sensibility that, beneath the differences between us, we find a commonality that makes mediation possible. Perhaps this is why we find between Gadamer and Derrida a philosophical engagement where, in a sense, the two never truly meet. In their famous Paris encounter of 1981[11] Derrida replies to Gadamer's account of "that experience [Erfahrung] that we all recognize" of understanding, with the comment: "I am not convinced that we ever really do have this experience that Professor Gadamer describes, of knowing in a dialogue that one has been perfectly understood or experiencing the success of confirmation."[12] With these words Derrida rejects the fundamental assumption upon which Gadamer's whole phenomenological account of understanding rests—that is, that understanding between people happens. Here Derrida, in his characteristic way, urges us to recognize that beneath what we think we understand wholly, completely, transparently and intelligibly are all sorts of breaks, confusions, and paradoxes (aporias). We must, from this perspective, leave our naiveté (or what Derrida might refer to as an overactive "good conscience") behind with regard to the possibility of a fusion of horizons, and realize that there are differences between us that cannot be reconciled or appropriated in understanding. It is only in this way, from the Derridean point of view, that we truly respect the Other, for only then do we truly recognize the robust individuality that is central to the Other's personhood. And, furthermore, only then do we recognize fully our own individuality and face up to the fact that we never really experience that "comfort" of being fully understood. In fact, from the Derridean point of view, we should always be weary of too much "comfort" in our communications, for it is probably a sign that we've assumed too much about the Other and ignored crucial signs of his otherness.

With Bernasconi's and Derrida's concerns in mind, let's consider more closely what the problem seems to be. Bernasconi had mentioned that "you don't know what I'm talking about" is something women say to men, something the oppressed say to the oppressor, and we can imagine that it is something that members of one culture might say to the members of a very different culture. Gadamer's response (and I think Bernasconi would agree) to the one who says "you don't know what I'm talking about" is likely to be: "I don't understand . . . yet!" Bernasconi is right to say that Gadamer is, in fact, committed to the notion that understanding is always in principle possible. Bernasconi is also right to say that this is because Gadamer sees there is always something present that fundamentally binds interlocutors: a common language (or translatable language) and a common subject matter or world. The most important point that I think Bernasconi is calling into question, in Gadamer's view of dialogue and understanding, is Gadamer's assumption that we really do always share a common subject matter with the Other. Bernasconi says: "To suppose that there is . . . a common theme or topic to be addressed, is to impose a hermeneutic model without listening to what is being said [by the one who declares you don't know what I'm talking about]."[13] We might ask the question in this way: What makes Gadamer think that he really shares a common subject matter with a woman without political or even reproductive rights in a poverty-stricken country, who is preparing to give birth without a midwife, without medication, and perhaps without any clean water? What makes Gadamer think he "shares a world" with this woman? What exactly would they talk about? What makes him think he could possibly come to know "what" she is talking about? When we put it this way, one can't help but wonder whether there isn't a real arrogance in Gadamer's claim that understanding is always in principle possible. We can't help but wonder whether, in order to make this claim, Gadamer must from the start imagine his Other in a form that is so familiar to him that he simultaneously must ignore or suppress what is truly different about the Other.

It is important to be clear about what Bernasconi's concern, here, really is. The one who says "you don't know what I'm talking about" is *not* saying "you don't know what it feels like to live my life" or "you can't experience what I experience." Bernasconi knows that knowing what it is like to *be* another person is not what Gadamer means by understanding (and Gadamer would simply agree that he can't know what its like to *be* anyone else). Understanding is not a matter of sharing some set of first-person experiences (*Erlebnisse*). Gadamer has been clear in his critique of Schleiermacher's hermeneutic model that the goal of understanding is not to get to know, or step into, the Other's life-experience, but to understand the content of what he says in language. This leads one to wonder whether Bernasconi's concern, surrounding the "agreement" that Gadamer says always takes place in understanding, is that Gadamer's agreement means not that we must reach a psychological agreement where we feel what the other feels, but rather that we must agree in our "judgment" on a particular topic in order to reach a shared understanding. If this is what Gadamer means when he says understanding always involves agreement, then it is a valid concern that Gadamer's pursuit of understanding is a pursuit that squelches dissent, or a variety of informed points of view on a shared topic. But this really isn't Bernasconi's concern either. Bernasconi knows that Gadamer's notion of the "agreement" that takes place in understanding is agreement over the subject matter, and not necessarily agreement in opinion. [14] Bernasconi shows that he recognizes this when he says that, when it comes to understanding one another according to Gadamer, "it may not be necessary to be of one mind with the other, but the goal is accord concerning the object." [15] He knows, then, that Gadamer's notion of agreement does not amount to having the same judgment as one's interlocutor, but can in fact mean "agreeing to disagree" in judgment, while still agreeing on what the content, or the crux of our disagreement is about. We might come to understand someone's counter-argument against us about a shared subject matter without finally agreeing with his judgment on the matter. A higher understanding would still develop between ourselves and the Other in dialogue if we take into consideration the Other's critical points, see the issue under discussion in new and surprising ways, becoming aware of problems that had not been noticed before, and integrate all the Other's insights into a more profound, self-critical grasp of the topic being considered. Yet, we may still, in the end, disagree with our interlocutor's judgment. In this case we may come to understand our interlocutor and reach an agreement with him on the subject matter, while ultimately disagreeing with him in opinion. [16] But, as tempting as it might be, to try to address Bernasconi's concern about understanding involving agreement by suggesting that Gadamer and the one who says "you don't know what I'm talking about" simply agree to disagree on the matter of whether or not understanding between them is in principle possible, this would miss the point of Bernasconi's criticism.

Bernasconi's real concern is that even the agreement to disagree presupposes a common subject matter about which we disagree. But it is this common subject matter, Bernasconi suggests, that may very well be missing between myself and the Other. Ignoring this possibility, and projecting onto the Other enough of a similarity to myself—enough of an overlapping world experience—to make it possible for me to understand what the Other is talking about means molding the Other into a "familiar" form (even before he speaks) in such a way that excludes the true alterity of the Other. Excluding the radical difference of the Other—a difference that might *really* call my old prejudices into question in a dramatic way—is not only a way of shielding myself from strangeness, but it is also a kind of suppression of, or violence done to, the Other. To truly recognize and respect the otherness of the Other, from Bernasconi's point of view, I should instead be open to the possibility of encountering something so strange that I find myself without a frame of reference into which I can integrate or understand it. A readiness for this kind of alterity would mean truly being open to having my old ways of thinking "shaken" by the Other. An acknowledgement of this kind of alterity would allow me to truly respect the otherness of the Other.

The charge against Gadamer—that is, that his model of understanding does not recognize the true alterity of the Other because it projects familiarity (by way of a shared subject matter, world, language) onto the Other from the start—offers an important warning about the Gadamerian model of dialogue and understanding. The charge compels us to remember that when we treat the Other as our "fellow partner" in dialogue, and we assume from the start that understanding the Other is always in principle possible, we run the risk of ignoring the things that really do separate us and make the Other dramatically or radically other. But furthermore, when we operate on the Gadamerian model of dialogue and understanding, we run the risk of fooling ourselves that the plight of understanding is always a fully respectful, happy, beneficial plight of social harmony in which a kind of "togetherness" is achieved. We should not fool ourselves into thinking that the project of understanding is always inclusive, when it in fact always involves some level of exclusion—exclusion of what remains so different that it cannot find a role in our game of understanding which requires, from the start, agreeing on so much: a language, a subject matter, a common question to answer, and so forth. We should not fool ourselves into believing that we ever achieve a kind of "complete" understanding with the Other where nothing is left out or ignored. We should not fool ourselves into thinking there is no dark side, no tragic side of exclusion, of the human journey of understanding.

These are important warnings that all Gadamerians should heed. But these warnings, I think, should ultimately not cause one to abandon the Gadamerian model of dialogue and understanding. It may be true that we can never *completely* understand the Other. It may also be true that we always run the risk of suppressing difference when we assume from the start that we will have *something* in common about which we can talk in order to get the process of understanding started. But we must be very careful about allowing these warnings to cause a sort of paralysis or withdrawal from dialogue in the face of the Other. These warnings should not cause us to give up the project of attempting to engage the Other and reach as much of an understanding as we can with him, for giving up on this project would have the most devastating sort of unethical consequences.

The most dangerous thing we could do is to interpret the critics' principle—the principle that there are differences between us that run so deep that we can never truly understand each Other—as a reason to no longer even *try* to understand those whose lives and ideas may be significantly different from our own. Although Derrida does not think his project leads to paralysis or a withdrawal from the project to understand, but sparks, instead, a new consideration of how and why it is that we never fully understand each other, I remain concerned that a withdrawal from trying to understand is a common consequence of thinking that we can't ever truly comprehend each other. When we assume from the start that we can never really understand where the Other is coming from, and that what the Other says will never be fully intelligible to us, we keep ourselves at a kind of distance that makes it impossible for the Other to speak meaningfully and affect our own understanding. This is an act of denying the Other the possibility of addressing us and challenging us which, as we have seen from the Gadamerian point of view, is a way of ignoring the Other and not taking seriously his claims to truth.[17]

By considering criticisms regarding the fate of "difference" in Gadamer's philosophy, we can conclude with a clearer sense of who the "Other" really is in philosophical hermeneutics, what sort of difference is recognized in the Other, and how that difference is treated. It is true that Gadamer's "Other" or "Thou" is one who shares with him, from the start, a remarkable amount: a common world, subject matter, and language. But this does not mean that the Other's difference is forgotten. Gadamer always recognizes that the Other is different in his embodied situation, his overall horizon of experience (*Erfahrung*), and his point of view that he can offer regarding the problems that concern us. These differences are welcomed as crucial contributions that fuel the open-ended process of understanding. Without some Other who introduces new meaning to us, there would be no play-movement of dialogue at all in which we enrich our grasp of the world together. Difference and tension, as we have seen, maintain a vital role in play, in that a certain amount of resistance is needed for there to be any game at all. In this way, every "playing with" is a "playing against" to a certain extent. The very motion of play needs a move and countermove, question and answer, call and response (we don't throw the ball if there's no one to throw it back). We don't learn anything unless there is something *other* confronting us and challenging our expectations and prejudices. The process of understanding is only *enriched* by the alterity of others who articulate their experiences and contribute to a heightened shared sense of the subject matter. Again, we can see that focusing on Gadamer's notion of understanding in terms of an ongoing game is a way of keeping the dynamic character of understanding in the foreground, and reminding us of the fact that all understanding involves the necessity of at least two *different* players participating in a back-and-forth movement. Difference or alterity is, in fact, the lifeblood of understanding. Dialogic play cannot occur without precisely the Other whose difference is appreciated as the force able to call our own understanding into question, and encourage us to rise above the nearsightedness of our grasp of the world and truly learn something. Attempting to do away with this alterity would mean attempting to stop the process of understanding—a process that, from the perspective of philosophical hermeneutics, is to be embraced as an activity that inevitably brings about our common human good.

What Gadamer's critics have made us recognize more fully is that the "difference" of the Other that is so important to philosophical hermeneutics is not a radically alien difference. It is a difference within the bounds of a common form of life—a *human* form of life. Because our Other is always different (within these bounds), his difference is always in principle understandable. Gadamer recognizes difference as "intelligible difference"—that is, as a difference that is not unreachable, but can be grasped in such a way that it can *make a difference to me.* This notion of difference as "intelligible difference" is what moves Gadamer to always listen to "the Other" with the famous "principle of charity" and assume that what the Other has to say will "make sense" if we exert the effort to listen and understand. For Gadamer the Other's difference remains always a "meaningful" difference, and I think that this is precisely what must be assumed if we are to offer the Other the sort of respect that makes us take his truth claims seriously. If we do not treat the Other's difference as being in principle intelligible, we risk emptying it of its meaningful content and reducing it to something formal and even trivial. If the "Other," and the Other's unique point of view, is taken to be something that I cannot ever grasp, then I worry that his individuality is reduced to a sort of formal difference (without content). It becomes simply a negation—"what I can't understand" or what is "not my grasp of things"—without having any positive meaning of its own. Reducing the Other to this sort of formal Other or simple "negative" is not a way of recognizing and respecting the *substantial* alternative the Other has to contribute to our own ways of thinking and living. Treating the Other as our "partner" in the play-process of understanding—as one who shares with us a basic form of life, but exists as a unique individual and offers us a fresh and challenging point of view—allows for the Thou to be approached with respect and understood to the fullest extent possible.

Treating the Other as "play-partner" does not entail abolishing or silencing difference. The Other's "intelligible" differences, in philosophical hermeneutics, are not treated as problems to be ignored, diminished, or smoothed over, but respected and preserved so that the open-ended shared game of understanding can continue.[18] The open-endedness of this game is important to emphasize. Understanding is never complete, according to Gadamer (a lesson we must take seriously if we fully recognize the finitude of human life). This means that even when a common understanding is developed that is so far reaching that it includes a deep agreement about a wide variety of subject matter (as might be the case with close friends), such an understanding is always susceptible to a new disagreement or rupture in understanding.[19] The type of frightening fusion that is often envisioned by Gadamer's critics—the kind that would close up the possibility of disagreement—is neither desirable nor is it really possible in the Gadamerian view. Gadamer stresses, against the Hegelian idea, that a final state of absolute knowledge cannot be reached. I and Thou will not finally reach a state where they agree about everything once and for all. In the ongoing, open-ended process of dialogic play and the unfolding of truth that occurs in it, there are stages of agreement, of reconciliation, and of shared understanding, which ultimately give way to new questions, new confusions, and new disagreements. As Gadamer's rather hopeful and optimistic philosophy of understanding teaches us, these ruptures, which occur in our efforts to grasp some subject matter, are themselves always open again to being bridged, mediated, and reconciled. But it is the oscillation of I and Thou on the back-and-forth journey of rupture and reconciliation,[20] that truly captures the open-ended play-process of understanding. If and when more "radical" types of difference assert themselves and we need to, with Derrida, consider what has been excluded from our game of understanding and move forward into an investigation of how and why we have never *fully* understood, we will still have to do this critical work in a dialogue in which we try to understand each other and reach agreements about the subject matter at hand. In order to enter into this dialogue, we will need to approach the Other with openness, stand "ready" to hear something new, "listen" to the Other's claim with seriousness, and "allow" that Other's claim to challenge and enrich our own thinking. We will, thus, need to practice the Gadamerian model of understanding in order to make progress together in such a new inquiry.[21]

It is this "open" manner of approaching the voice of the Other who speaks to us either face to face or across time that allows one to show the Other the highest level of respect and make the most progress with him in the dialogical quest for understanding. The open approach to the Other, thus, marks the most genuine of I-Thou relations, for Gadamer, and characterizes the true hermeneutic experience in which our understanding and self-understanding is transformed. It is this comportment of openness toward the Other that constitutes a crucial ethical condition for the possibility of genuine dialogue in which interlocutors may come to understand each other about some subject matter and share some truth about their world.

NOTES

1. In James Risser's book, *Hermeneutics and the Voice of the Other*, Risser calls philosophical hermeneutics itself a "hermeneutics of the voice" and rightly recognizes that it is a hermeneutics in which there is always an "emphasis on the other" (James Risser, *Hermeneutics and the Voice of the Other* [Albany: SUNY Press, 1997], 15). Understanding, whether of an artwork, text, of other form of tradition is an understanding of the voice of the Other.

2. It is important, I think, that we not jump to the conclusion that Gadamer is a clear Kantian when it comes to ethics. Gadamer's mode of thinking the ethical is much closer to Aristotle, as we will discuss in chapter 8. We should see the role of "treating the Other as an end (a human being) and not a means (an object to be used)" in Gadamer's philosophy to be less of an a priori rule, and more of a guiding principle that we derive from experience. From experience we know that treating the Other in this manner is a mode of respect, and we also know, from experience, that it has a positive effect on interpersonal relations, allowing human beings to function in their interactions at their highest (and deepest) levels.

3. Related to Habermas's critique of Gadamer's notion of understanding—which he says involves a kind of submission to the powerful authority of tradition—is Habermas's sense that Gadamer has forgotten, or is generally insensitive to, the category of power. Habermas charges Gadamer with neglecting the extra-linguistic forces that shape the context of thought and conversation, and with not recognizing the conditions of power upon which the possibility of genuine dialogue and understanding depend. In his "Review of *Truth and Method*," he instructs Gadamer in the fact that language "is a medium of domination and social power; it serves to legitimate relations of organized force" and that a kind of hermeneutics that recognizes the *conditions* upon which genuine communication depends (which Gadamer's does not) "changes into critique of ideology" (Jürgen Habermas, "Review of *Truth and Method*," in *The Hermeneutic Tradition: From Ast to Ricoeur*, eds. Gayle L. Ormiston and Alan D. Schrift [Albany: SUNY Press, 1990], 239–40). In Habermas's essay "The Hermeneutic Claim to Universality," he goes on to explain that there are numerous ways in which our communication becomes "systematically distorted" where there is a false appearance of "understanding each other," and a false appearance of the "agreement" or "consensus" that is involved in understanding each other (Habermas, "The Hermeneutic Claim to Universality," in *The Hermeneutic Tradition: From Ast to Ricoeur*, eds. Gayle L. Ormiston and Alan D. Schrift [Albany: SUNY Press, 1990], 252–54, 266–70). In these cases, interlocutors are caught up in an uneven power dynamic, of which they may not even be aware, which makes *real* consensus (which would have to be between equals) impossible. In such cases, what is needed is an "external observer" who is able to detect and diagnose (as a psychoanalyst would) the distortion and its causes. Because Gadamer's hermeneutics is an account of nondistorted communicative understanding, Habermas feels that its domain is limited (and not universal, as Gadamer declares), and that a critical theory is needed to go beyond philosophical hermeneutics and act as that "external observer" mentioned.

In response to Habermas's criticism that Gadamer does not recognize the conditions of power that make or break genuine dialogue, I would argue that—though it is true that Gadamer does not discuss *all* the different ways that communication is distorted in contemporary society—he is not completely ignorant of the conditions of power equality that are necessary for genuine dialogue and understanding to occur. He, with considerable effort, describes three instances in which the interpreter tries to overpower the other in conversation—that is, in the *scientific* approach to the Other, where one tries to know the Other as a natural thing, the *psychological* approach to the Other, which aims to know the other's mind, life, and intentions better than he knows himself, and (as we will see in chapter 6) the *sophistic* approach to the Other, in which one aims to beat the other in an argument. Gadamer, thus, shows us that he too is concerned with "distorted" dialogues in which power relations are thrown off balance so that genuine dialogue and understanding is never achieved. The problem with all three of these distorted dialogues is a lack of ethical conditions—a shared openness to the Other and their claim to truth—which results in the "I" not treating his "Thou" (interlocutor) as an equal partner in the game of understanding, and the dialogue breaking down.

4. This is something the previous two approaches toward understanding the Other (the scientific and psychological approaches) seemed to miss, for they naively sought after a kind of "objective" knowledge that involved transcending historical situatedness. (The scientific approach thought it could reach a pure objective knowledge of human nature, untainted by the interpretive standpoint of the scientist [something we discussed in depth in chapter 1], and the psychological approach thought that it could transcend the investigator's own set of life experiences in order to step into the mind and life of the Other.)

5. Remember that Gadamer explained that the past speaks to us via tradition as a genuine partner in dialogue—as a "Thou." The fusion of horizons between past and present that occurs in our understanding of tradition is already understood by Gadamer as a fusion between the I of the present and the Thou of the past. But as

understanding can also take place between an I and Thou who both live in the present, the fusion of horizons can also refer to what happens when two people understand each other in living dialogue.

6. I am borrowing from Habermas the useful distinction between the vertical and horizontal senses of communication. Gadamer's hermeneutics aims to achieve communicative understanding in both directions. See Habermas, "Review," 232.

7. One can get a better sense of how frightening and violent the image of fusion can appear if one imagines the fusing power of, say, Star Trek's "Borg," who terrifyingly attempt to eliminate all individuality and difference by "assimilating" independent persons into their "collective." Whether you are the one being assimilated, or the one doing the assimilating in fusion, the image is a horror to anyone who cares about respecting individuals.

8. Robert Bernasconi, "'You Don't Know What I'm Talking About': Alterity and the Hermeneutic Ideal," in *The Specter of Relativism*, ed. Lawrence Schmidt (Evanston, Ill.: Northwestern University Press, 1995), 192.

9. Bernasconi, "Alterity and the Hermeneutic Ideal," 192.

10. Bernasconi, "Alterity and the Hermeneutic Ideal," 193.

11. This encounter is published in Diane P. Michelfelder and Richard E. Palmer, eds., *Dialogue and Deconstruction: The Gadamer-Derrida Encounter* (Albany: SUNY Press, 1989).

12. Michelfelder and Palmer eds., *Dialogue and Deconstruction*, 54.

13. Bernasconi, "Alterity and the Hermeneutic Ideal," 192–93.

14. There is a debate within Gadamer scholarship about what Gadamer really means by the "agreement" that always takes place in understanding. Georgia Warnke offers a helpful analysis of the ambiguity present in Gadamer's term "agreement," which he sometimes uses to refer to "a unity of judgment" (or a consensus), but other times uses to refer to "a reflective and critical integration" in which we might agree to disagree over the subject matter. (Georgia Warnke, *Gadamer: Hermeneutics, Tradition and Reason* [Stanford: Stanford University Press, 1987], 102–6). Bernasconi's concern does not seem to be about the unity of judgment, as he seems to recognize that Gadamer talks about agreement in the looser sense of agreeing over the subject matter without "being of one mind" about it. Bernasconi's concern seems to be over whether we really always have that shared subject matter about which we can talk.

15. Bernasconi, "Alterity and the Hermeneutic Ideal," 180.

16. One should take caution not to conflate the agreement over the subject matter that happens when we understand someone with agreement in opinion. We should not fear the possibility of coming to an understanding with someone because we are terrified that this would mean having to share their opinion (as some feel about the prospect of understanding a bigot or terrorist). Listening to each others' articulations of the subject matter can only further enrich our understanding. Understanding what another says and recognizing what is true in it does not entail agreeing about everything with him. It does not necessarily entail, for instance, feeling the way he feels about it or judging it the way he does.

17. I sense, from his frustrated response to Derrida, that Gadamer himself feels that Derrida has reserved for himself the kind of distance in their encounter that makes it impossible for him to receive Gadamer's address, believing from the start that they will not understand each other, and thus making any real dialogue or mutual development in their understanding impossible as well. Gadamer suggests in his reply to Derrida that while he has tried to respond to Derridean concerns and truly address Derrida in his own lecture, and while he continues to try to foster a better understanding between himself and Derrida, that Derrida himself does not have this goal in mind. He states of Derrida: "Is he really disappointed that we cannot understand each other? Indeed not, for in his view this would be a relapse into metaphysics. He will, in fact, be pleased, because he takes this private experience of disillusionment to confirm his own metaphysics" (Michelfelder and Palmer eds., *Dialogue and Deconstruction*, 56). No enriched understanding takes place in their encounter, Gadamer suggests, because

Derrida does not try or want for this to happen, which conveniently confirms his own view that no genuine understanding *can* happen. I take this whole episode to be a confirmation of my thesis in this section: that genuine understanding relies upon a shared ethical commitment between interlocutors to try to understand each other.

18. For an excellent discussion of the "respect for others" that is essential to the open approach to the Other and genuine hermeneutic understanding, see Lawrence Schmidt's article "Respecting Others: The Hermeneutic Virtue," *Continental Philosophy Review* 33, no. 3 (July 2000): 359–79. Schmidt shows how a "respect for others" has been a central concern throughout Gadamer's philosophical career.

19. This may be where Gadamer and Derrida come nearest to each other in their visions of the possibilities and limits of understanding.

20. Richard Bernstein, in his essay "Reconciliation/Rupture" (in *The New Constellation: The Ethical-Political Horizons of Modernity/Postmodernity* [Cambridge: MIT Press, 1991]), responds to the tendency of modern and postmodern thinkers to emphasize one or the other of this "Either/Or." Taking Hegel as a great advocate of reconciliation as the finale of spirit, and his critics as those who stress the ruptures of human existence that can never be bridged, healed, or mediated, Bernstein takes the position with regard to them that it is only in accounting for the reality and significance of both sides of reconciliation/rupture that we fully understand our human form of life. Because Gadamer emphasizes the *open-ended* dialogue that constitutes our human way of life, I believe that Gadamer does just this.

21. While Gadamer's critics argue that there is an important limit to the kind of difference that Gadamer acknowledges and respects in his theory of understanding, we can't help but find ourselves pulled back into the Gadamerian dialogue as soon as we try to cross over the limit and discuss what kind of difference that might be. Because of this, the very inquiry into the limits of philosophical hermeneutics seems to take place according to a hermeneutic model.

Chapter 6

Genuine Play in Action: The Model of the Philosopher

In Gadamer's discussion of the "open" approach to the Other, we saw that the process of genuine dialogue and understanding always begins with *risking* our own prejudices, or "*bringing* them into play" so that we have a chance to correct and revise them. Risking our own prejudices is the necessary beginning to any inquiry. In order to ask a first question about some subject matter, we have to acknowledge that our understanding is incomplete and likely flawed, and be willing to test what we think we know. In other words, in order to ask a question and open up a process of learning, we have to be willing to make our own thinking "questionable." The question is the starting point of any hermeneutic experience. It is the question, Gadamer explains, that breaks open or brings into the open the subject matter that is to be interrogated. It also determines the scope and limits of what will count as a meaningful answer. Because of this, Gadamer sees the question as taking priority in all understanding and claims that "the path of all knowledge leads through the question" (TM, 363). For Gadamer, the ultimate model that displays the proper structure of inquiry is the dialectical dialogue, and the exemplary figure who embodies the comportment of openness that is crucial for its success is none other than the quintessential philosopher himself: Socrates.

Socratic dialectic—that truth-seeking enterprise by which interlocutors in Plato's dialogues attempt to "give an account" of the true meaning of (usually) some ethical term—proceeds by way of question and answer. We learn well from Socrates that nothing is to be found without our "seeking" and that no knowledge can ever be gained unless we first ask a question. But we also learn from Socrates that no question will be asked without a *desire* to know, which in turn relies on a particular stance that the inquirer must take. In order to desire to know, one has to already acknowledge that one does not already know. This is the stance represented in Socrates' famous assertion that his only knowledge is of his own ignorance: the one thing he knows is that he knows nothing. Socrates' great mission, to persuade his fellow citizens to care for the health of their souls above all else and to seek knowledge, had to begin, then, by sparking in his interlocutors that same realization that knowledge was lacking, which would in turn inspire the desire to know. Socrates aimed to bring about this experience of a *lack* through the sting of his famous mode of refutation (*elenchus*), which served to throw his interlocutors back upon themselves in confusion, open up a space of questionability, arouse a desire to seek answers, and drive them into the genuine dialectical investigation leading toward knowledge. Socrates' *elenchus*, as a productive mode of refutation, inspired in his interlocutors the stance of perplexity and humility needed to desire knowledge and begin with Socrates a joint inquiry into the truth of the matter under discussion.

Socrates' first task was to inspire in his interlocutors a first questioning or, in other words, *a first opening to truth*. The Socratic dialectic, Gadamer states, "is reserved to the person who wants to know—i.e., who already has questions. The art of questioning is not the art of resisting the pressure of opinion; it already presupposes this freedom" (TM, 366). Dialectic is for those who are *already open* to the possible questionableness of their own opinions, and those willing to find out about a truth that might contradict their previously held beliefs. But because this dialectic is an activity that always occurs in and through dialogue and is an "account giving" of truth that always involves giving and receiving that account *to and from another person* in conversation, the inquirer must not only display an *openness to truth* but also an *openness to the other person* with whom a *genuine dialogue* can be carried out.

SOCRATES VERSUS THE SOPHISTS

The art of dialectic is, Gadamer claims, "the art of conducting a real dialogue" (TM, 367). This *real* or *authentic* dialogue is contrasted by Gadamer with the inauthentic conversation popularly conducted by the sophists, when he states that "the art of dialectic is not the art of being able to win every argument" (TM, 367). The kind of inauthentic dialogue presented by Plato as dangerously rampant in the ancient world was the sort engaged in for the purpose of defeating one's interlocutor in argument, but not for the ultimate purpose of gaining insight. The sophists, as Plato presents them, approach conversation as a contest (*agon*) with no further aim than winning arguments and acquiring the honor, money, and power granted the victor. On the other hand, the Socratic dialogue is driven by the continual attempt not to outdo each other but to reach agreement at every step in the argument, so that there is certainty that both interlocutors always know *what* they are discussing—that is, so that there is always a common subject matter being worked through. The interlocutors in a genuine Socratic dialogue, who engage each other in a true philosophic spirit, keep their eye on what they consider to be the real prize of their conversation: the subject matter and its unfolding *truth*.

Plato's depiction of the sophists provides us with a particularly good example of those who listen to their interlocutor only for the purpose of discovering the vulnerable moment in their speech upon which they may be refuted. This is not the genuine listening that we described as constituting a true openness to the Other, in which the Thou's words are taken seriously as a claim to truth from which we might learn. The Sophist, instead, remains always at a safe competitive distance from his interlocutors' claims, and guards himself against being affected by the possible truth of his opponent's words. In the sophistic approach to the Other, we have actually uncovered a third form of "foul play" (in addition to the scientific and psychological approaches already examined) that can help us illuminate what is so distinctive about genuine play. With the Sophist we find a third form of "closedness to the Other," and a third I-Thou relation in which a real consideration of the Other's claim to truth is avoided.

Conversation for a sophist, as it tends to be represented by Plato, is entered into in the spirit of "attack and conquer," where one aims to see only how one's interlocutor might be wrong, rather than in the spirit of collaborative learning in which one tries to understand how his dialogue partner might be right. Socratic dialectic, on the other hand, "consists in not trying to discover the weakness of what is said, but in bringing out its real strength. It is not the art of arguing (which can make a strong case out of a weak one) but the art of thinking (which can strengthen objections by referring to the subject matter)" (TM, 367). The Socratic dialectic allows for opinions to truly be tested, so that their legitimacy or illegitimacy may emerge, and so ungrounded beliefs can be transformed into knowledge.

By turning to the model of Socratic dialectical dialogue and the figure of Socrates, in comparison with the sophists, we see that entering into a true dialogue means comporting oneself with both an openness and directedness toward the Other, and also with an openness and directedness toward truth itself as the ultimate goal. The interlocutors must *want* and *try* to understand each other and *want* and *try* to know the truth. They must then, share what Gadamer calls a *good will*[1] to understand each other and to grasp truth as an ultimate goal or an ultimate *good*. In other words, interlocutors must be open to each other and open to *the good*. To get a better understanding of this double openness that is necessary for knowledge to occur, I want to take a closer look at the model of Socratic dialogue that is presented to us by Plato, in which Gadamer's work is deeply rooted. This will give us a richer understanding of the ethical conditions of understanding that we find emerging from Gadamer's work.

THE DOUBLE OPENNESS OF AN ETHICAL FRIENDSHIP

Turning to Plato's dialogues allows us to dig deeper into the subtleties of the openness that constitutes a crucial ethical condition of the knowledge that emerges in dialectical dialogue. In this discussion I aim to illuminate the special kind of relationship between interlocutors—a relationship I would like to call an "ethical friendship"[2]—upon which this dialogical endeavor depends. By now we can see that a genuine dialogue is not simply the activity of two voices speaking about a shared topic—though this is an essential part of it. A genuine dialogue, in which coming to knowledge is a real possibility, can only take place if both interlocutors (1) share a reciprocal openness toward each other, in which they are willing to speak, listen, and respond to one another in a careful, cooperative, and sincere manner that facilitates understanding, and (2) share a mutual openness and general directedness toward truth as an ultimate good. In other words, they must share a desire, care, and quest for truth as an ultimate goal, which drives their joint endeavor.

The fact that *any* kind of dialogue requires, at the very least, enough of a reciprocal openness toward one another that both parties are willing to speak and listen to each other, becomes painfully clear in the opening lines of Plato's *Republic*. As Socrates and Glaucon are returning to town from Piraeus, Polemarchus, son of Cephalus, threatens (however playfully) to detain Socrates with the help of his friends by force, unless he is able to prove stronger than them. When Socrates suggests that there is an alternative to a contest of force when attempting to influence others' actions—that is, the alternative of *persuasion*—Polemarchus asks him a fateful question: "But could you persuade us," he said, "if we refuse to listen."[3] Here we are made aware of the glaring fact that if Socrates' potential interlocutors refuse to listen, and so close themselves off from the process of dialogue and its guiding power (or worse, silence Socrates by force), then his great mission to persuade his fellow Athenians to care for the well-being of their souls above all else, and to turn them toward a search for truth, is rendered hopeless. This harsh truth that Socrates must face remains our truth as well. If those we encounter are unwilling to talk to us and listen to us, no genuine dialogue in which we can improve our knowledge together can take place. There must be at least a minimal comportment of openness toward one another—a minimal level of respect for each other that enables two people to have a verbal exchange—for any dialogue to get started.

But, in addition, interlocutors must display, at least, that minimal comportment of openness toward truth that is involved in making an inquiry and asking a question. Any real discussion or search for the meaning of justice, virtue and the like, must begin, as mentioned, with the asking of a question. But the asking of a question presupposes an awareness that one doesn't yet know what one wants to know and that one has something to learn. Now, the attitude of perplexity and humility, as said, is something Socrates continually shows us that he possesses himself, and is also something he is always eager to inspire in others by helping them to realize that they are lacking the moral knowledge that is most important for health and happiness in their lives. We see Socrates' eagerness to inspire the attitude of perplexity and humility when Socrates, in Plato's *Meno*, replies to Meno's accusation that Socrates stings his interlocutors like a torpedo fish when he questions them in dialogue and makes them feel paralyzed and confused with regard to what they thought they understood. Socrates responds by explaining that the perplexity he inspires has a positive function, and uses Meno's slave boy as an example of this fact. After questioning the slave boy about a geometrical problem, Socrates says to Meno regarding his slave:

> At first he did not know what the basic line of the eight-foot square was; even now he does not yet know, but then he thought he knew, and answered confidently as if he did know, and he did not think himself at a loss, but now he does think himself at a loss, and as he does not know, neither does he think he knows . . . now, as he does not know, he would be glad to find out. . . . Do you think that before he would have tried to find out that which he thought he knew though he did not, before he fell into perplexity and realized he did not know and longed to know?[4]

Socrates shows Meno that it is only through becoming perplexed that one can open oneself up to a real inquiry, since it is only then that one is willing to ask a question and be lead by the course of the conversation. The sting of Socrates' refutation (*elenchus*) is essential for producing a stance in one's interlocutors that will allow them to *open* to the journey toward truth.

Now, not only must there be a basic openness of interlocutors toward one another and toward truth for the movement of dialogue to reach the heights sought by Socrates, but also a *deeper friendship* toward both must be developed. The movement of dialogue, which is governed by the rule of reaching agreement at each step of the conversation, requires a reciprocal *cooperative stance* of interlocutors toward each other. This cooperative stance that Socrates strives for with his interlocutors in Plato's dialogues is just what Gadamer has been articulating as a crucial condition of understanding throughout his *Truth and Method*. It involves making an effort to listen to what one's partner is saying, exercising a good will to understand him, taking what is said seriously and worthy of examination, finding a common ground and defining common terms, articulating and rearticulating positions so that they are understandable to one's partner, being sensitive to the other person's progress, and actively asking questions so that the other's words are clarified. The one who is willing and able to approach his partner in such a patient yet persistent manner—the one who makes a commitment to treating his interlocutor in a way that is

conducive to dialogue—displays a real care for his interlocutor's understanding and proves to be the genuine friend. Fostering knowledge for
himself and his interlocutor through dialogue, the friend cares *in deed* for
his partner's highest well-being, assuming with Socrates that knowledge
is the greatest good for the soul. A care for the Other's understanding goes
hand in hand with a care for truth, and a genuine friendship with the
Other goes hand in hand with a friendship with wisdom (*philosophia*).
What we understand as an ethical friendship must include both interlocutors' reciprocal care for each other, and their mutual care for "the good."[5]

In Plato's *Meno* we can see Socrates trying to cultivate such an ethical
friendship with Meno (though his success at doing so is questionable).
While trying to explain to Meno what it means to give a definition of a
term, and articulate its "form," Socrates explicitly states that discovering
common terms is an essential aspect of any inquiry, and that *friends*,
unlike "disputations debaters," make arguments and explanations in
terms that can be understood by one another. When asked by Meno what
he would do if his definition turned out to utilize another term unknown
to his interlocutor, Socrates answers: "If my questioner was one of those
clever and disputatious debaters, I would say to him: 'I have given my
answer; if it is wrong, it is your job to refute it.'" On the other hand, if
interlocutors "are friends as you and I are, and want to discuss with each
other, they must answer in a manner more gentle and more proper to
discussion. By this I mean that the answers must not only be true, but in
terms admittedly known to the questioner."[6] Socrates attempts to show
Meno that a dialogue in which truth can really be sought is one where
interlocutors (a) approach each other in a manner that fosters mutual
understanding, and (b) are both directed toward truth as the goal of their
discussion. Those "disputatious debaters" or sophists of which Socrates
speaks, by contrast, care only to refute each other for refutation's sake, or
for the sake of winning the argument and the reputation earned by
overpowering another in speech, and not for the sake of finding out what
is really true as a guide for their lives.

The character of Thrasymachus in the first book of the *Republic*
represents a classic example of such a "disputatious debater" and the sort
of comportment toward one's interlocutor and toward truth that is unfit
for genuine dialogue. Thrasymachus pounces on the argument in the
manner of a rabid dog, shouting at Socrates and Polemarchus and calling
them fools who "make way for each other."[7] He is quick to spout a slogan
to define what justice is—that it is "nothing other than the advantage of
the stronger"—without any interest in a back-and-forth movement with
his listeners in which his slogan might be clarified and tested, and without
any care for whether or not his listeners understand what he has said or
have learned anything. When pressed by Socrates and the others to
elaborate on what he means, Thrasymachus resists Socrates' usual ques-
tion-and-answer style, making personal attacks at every turn (calling

Socrates a sycophant and a child with a sniveling nose), and finally making an uninterrupted speech in the familiar sophist's style. After he has given his speech, Socrates tells us, he "had it in mind to go away, just like a bathman, after having poured a great shower of speech into our ears all at once."[8] Socrates accuses Thrasymachus of having no concern for the well-being of his fellow citizens to whom he speaks, nor any care for the truth, and presses him to make an effort to give an account of his position and truly persuade him and the others that justice is the advantage of the stronger. Thrasymachus though—proving that he has no interest in testing his own argument's truth and that he has no interest in treating his interlocutors in a way that would foster their understanding—responds to Socrates by saying: "And how shall I persuade you? If you're not persuaded by what I've just now said, what more shall I do for you? Shall I take the argument and give your soul a forced feeding?"[9] Thrasymachus lacks the ability to be a genuine partner in dialogue, for he cares only for his private interest at others' expense, that is, his reputation for winning at the humiliation of his opponents, and has no interest in the truth of his arguments and their effect on the lives they guide, for better or for worse. The ethical friendship necessary for the truth of justice to unfold in dialogue cannot be forged with Thrasymachus, and he is ultimately left behind in the conversation, while Glaucon and Adeimantus take center stage.[10]

Now, it is true, Socrates also can be found utilizing the art of refutation and what might appear at first glance to be simple sophistic tricks. But his refutation is educational in its essence. The Socratic *elenchus* is not refutation for its own sake—for the sake of winning the argument—but for the sake of that inquiry-opening perplexity of which we spoke. It is for the purpose of turning souls toward truth and is, thus, out of a true care for the well-being of Socrates' fellow interlocutors, whose souls are benefited through the truth-seeking endeavor. Socrates even explicitly says to Meno, upon whom he uses his famous *elenchus*, that he converses with him "for [Meno's] sake and [his] own" and that, in regard to showing Meno the truth, he is "willing to do [his] best for [Meno's] sake."[11] Socrates shows himself to be a friend to Meno, caring for his progress, patiently leading him in the discussion, and trying to cultivate in him both the attitude of friendship toward his interlocutor that is necessary for their dialogic quest to take place, as well as a genuine friendship with wisdom. He encourages Meno, when faced with Meno's suggestion that truth cannot be sought if one doesn't know what one is looking for, to have the attitude that the discovery of truth *is* possible and that searching for it is worthwhile. Socrates tells him that "we will be better men, braver and less idle, if we believe that one must search for the things one does not know, rather than if we believe that it is not possible to find out what we do not know and that we must not look for it."[12]

Socrates knows well that refuting one's interlocutor is not the proper end of a genuine discussion, but is merely the beginning, and a tool used to open up a common desire to learn something. He expresses this dramatically after his famous battle with Thrasymachus at the end of Book I of the *Republic*—which depicts Socrates (as Thrasymachus puts it) "feasting on the argument" and caught up in refuting Thrasymachus— when Socrates states that he has not had a fine banquet and has not yet learned what justice is. Here Plato is able to show us clearly that Socrates is not a sophist, for refutation and winning are not his highest goals, nor his highest sources of satisfaction. They serve as a mere preliminary to genuine dialogue, as we see in the structure of the *Republic* itself, for it is only at the end of Book I—once Socrates has had a chance to show that the methods of the sophist do not yield knowledge, to earn the respect of his interlocutors, and to spark a real desire in them to know what justice is— that we see the upward-moving dialogue of the text begin. It is only once Socrates is able to forge a genuine friendship with his interlocutors, or at least plant the seeds of such a friendship that will inevitably blossom throughout the conversation, that the kind of dialogue for which he strives can proceed. It is through, on the one hand, the main interlocutors' desire to understand each other, their concern for each other's under-standing, and their spirit of cooperation, and on the other hand their active questioning and their inquiry into the subject matter, that makes possible the heights of the dialogical and educational journey achieved by Socrates, Glaucon, and Adeimantus. In other words, it is the interlocutors' genuine openness toward each other and toward truth that makes the upward movement of understanding possible. The condition for the possibility of the knowledge sought by Socrates—a knowledge whose very mode of existence is a living, genuine dialogue—is a shared ethics: a shared value in and care for the education and well-being of each other's soul, and a shared value in and care for truth as the ultimate nourishment for the soul.

Gadamer, whose own work is influenced deeply by the Socratic model of dialogue as presented by Plato, appropriates this message in his own philosophy of understanding, and hands down to us the insight that ethical conditions must be met if any knowledge of any truth is to occur. We have found that true participation in the game of understanding requires a host of "commitments," "accomplishments," or "tasks" on the parts of the players. These include letting the other speak, listening, sensitivity to the alterity of what the Other says, recognition of and responsiveness to the Other's claim to truth, allowing the Thou to address us, asking questions, readiness to examine and revise our own prejudices, risking false assumptions, and readiness for self-transformation. All of these serve to generate and sustain the essential comportment of "open-ness" that marks the highest of I-Thou relations. We cannot help but recognize, and Gadamer is happy to remind us, that these tasks are commonly avoided, refused, ignored, or passed over in a way that results in a failure to truly encounter the Other, in the degeneration of dialogue, and in a breakdown of understanding. It is easy to close ourselves off from the Other, ignore the Other and his claim to truth, stubbornly resist being affected, or overhastily assimilate what he says to our own expectations of meaning. It is easy for us to perform monologues alongside each other under the illusion that we are having a real interaction. It is easy to psychoanalyze the Other and listen to what he has to say in terms of a personal point of view, an expression of his private life experience, but not an articulation of some truth worthy of serious consideration. It is easy to reject the tasks of true play and of real engagement, in exchange for the tasks of disengagement required by modern science for achieving the so-called objective knowledge that it seeks. But objectifying the Other is a sure way, according to Gadamer, to fail at our chance to reach a genuine understanding with him. Finally, it is easy to become caught up in a desire to outsmart our interlocutor or "beat him" in the argument, and lose sight of the purpose of understanding some truth that is emerging in the conversation. In the face of the temptation to slide into these various types of degenerate dialogue, we will have to embrace the work and the self-discipline it will take to sustain the comportment of openness to the Other that is necessary for genuine dialogue and understanding to take place. In other words, as Gadamer has shown us following the Socratic tradition, all real knowledge relies upon ethical conditions that are *up to us* to realize.

NOTES

1. Gadamer's notion that all understanding relies upon a "good will" to understand is another point of contention between Gadamer and Derrida. In their Paris encounter, Derrida raises the question of Nietzsche and the psychoanalytic tradition of interpretation, asking what role the "good will" could possibly have in their type of work (Diane P. Michelfelder and Richard E. Palmer, eds., *Dialogue and Deconstruction: The Gadamer-Derrida Encounter* [Albany: SUNY Press, 1989], 53). This question presents a sort of face-off between the project of interpretation undertaken by (what Ricoeur called) "the hermeneutics of suspicion," which aims always at interpretation by way of "unmasking," and Gadamer's "hermeneutics of trust," which focuses not on the subjective motivation or intention of the speaker, but on the subject matter or content of the conversation. In light of that "will to power," which Nietzsche taught us penetrates and lurks behind all interpretations of truth, and, thus, forms a whole layer of meaning and intention behind *what* is said that must be brought to light and taken into account, the question arises as to whether or not the idea of a "good will to understand" is simply naïve. If *what* is said is simply a mask of one's will to power, and a tool for gaining power over the Other, then approaching what the Other says with "good will" means immediately submitting to his control. We cannot assume the "sincerity" of the Other, nor can we assume it in our own supposed "good efforts" to understand (which likely mask a deeper will to power as well). If we want to truly understand what someone says, we need—according to the Nietzscheans—to get back behind his words to his motivations, and analyze how his so-called claim to truth is working to create or

maintain his domination. What I have tried to show, as it relates to this debate, is that—far from being *naively unaware* of the possibility that interlocutors might harbor intentions *other* than the "good will to understand"—Gadamer shows us that these other intentions must be *set aside* if a shared, genuine understanding of the subject matter is to be developed. Gadamer knows well that a "good will" to understand one another is not always present, for he is keenly aware, for instance, of the existence of sophists all around us. But his whole point is that these sophists, who lack the good will to understand and aim to overpower their interlocutor in an argument, might emerge the "victor" of a contest, but will never truly enrich their understanding. Now we may be tempted—along with those hermeneuts of suspicion—to embark on a project of psychoanalysis in order to show that the sophist's true goal in conversation is winning rather than grasping truth. But the Gadamerian lesson is that this still will not bring forth any genuine shared understanding of truth with him; for the work of unmasking, as we already saw in Gadamer's critique of the psychological approach to the Other, is a way of "mastering" the Other in "knowing him better than he knows himself," and not coming to a shared grasp of truth.

2. By "ethical friendship" I mean "true" friendship. The lesson that Socrates teaches us time and again is that the only true friendship is the one in which there is a reciprocal care for each other's knowledge, virtue, and general well-being, and the one in which there is a mutual love of truth. We may, as Aristotle explicitly notes in his *Nicomachean Ethics*, call other reciprocal relationships "friendships"—namely, those relationships where we exchange with each other something we want or need (e.g., business associates) and/or take some common interest or pleasure in something (e.g., tennis buddies). But these relationships do not represent, by Socrates' standards (or Aristotle's), the highest kind of friendship, because they lack the *ethical* aspect mentioned.

3. Plato, *The Republic of Plato*, ed. and trans. Allan Bloom (New York: Basic Books, 1968), 327c.

4. Plato, *Meno*, in *Five Dialogues: Euthyphro, Apology, Crito, Meno, Phaedo*, trans. G. M. A. Grube (Indianapolis and Cambridge: Hackett Publishing Compay, 1981), 84a–c.

5. The openness and directedness toward one another and toward truth intimately belong together and are two sides of the same coin that I want to call the genuine ethical friendship. There can be no genuine relationship between interlocutors, no reciprocal friendship with each other in which there is a care for each other's understanding and well-being, without also a genuine relationship with, and directedness toward the good. In other words, there can be no real friendship with one another unless both partners also have a friendship with wisdom (*philosophia*) and strive for truth as the ultimate nourishment and highest good for the soul. Likewise, any real friendship with wisdom and quest for truth requires a genuine partner in dialogue with whom to embark on the truth-seeking endeavor in speech. The philosophical journey, thus, requires an interlocutor who cares about our progress and well-being.

This is shown well in Socrates' second speech in the *Phaedrus*, where he explains that the friend of wisdom can only regain his wings and his knowledge in and through a loving friendship with another and their shared "orderly life and friendship with wisdom" (Plato, *Phaedrus* in *Plato's Erotic Dialogues*, trans. William S. Cobb [Albany: SUNY Press, 1993], 256a–b). In addition, it is only the friend of wisdom that proves to be the true friend and worthy lover, since he is the one who encourages his lover to engage in what is truly good for his soul—the dialogical search for truth. Socrates—the philosopher and the partner who will not allow Phaedrus to become bewitched by the falsity of Lysias' speech and miss out on noble love and real wisdom—proves to be the true friend to Phaedrus.

6. Plato, *Meno*, 75c–d.

7. Plato, *Republic*, 336c.

8. Plato, *Republic*, 344d.

9. Plato, *Republic*, 345b. It is worth noting, again—for the benefit of all "hermeneuts of suspicion" who believe that Gadmer has no sense of the category of power—that Gadamer knows well, from his grounding in Plato, that force plays a central role in

degenerate dialogue, and must be eliminated in genuine dialogue if knowledge is to develop. In a genuine dialogue interlocutors must listen, speak, respond, agree, and disagree freely for the discussion to move forward on the strength of the reasons given for each position.

10. Kenneth Seeskin, in his book *Dialogue and Discovery*, rightly remarks: "Genuine speech requires more than linguistic competence. Arrogance, conceit, and hostility—all the vices which threaten social harmony also threaten conversation. To the degree that they threaten conversation, they hinder philosophical discovery" (Kenneth Seeskin, *Dialogue and Discovery: A Study in Socratic Method* [Albany: SUNY Press, 1987], 23). Thrasymachus, embodying these vices, acts as an obstacle to the progress that friends are able to accomplish in dialogue, and is an obstacle that must be somehow overcome for such an upward movement to occur. Socrates is able to make way for a genuine inquiry with Glaucon and Adeimantus only by first "taming the beast," so to speak, which he does when he inevitably causes Thrasymachus to blush.

11. Plato, *Meno*, 77a, 82a.

12. Plato, *Meno*, 86b–c.

Chapter 7

The Value of Genuine Play: Transition to Play as a Guide to Life

Our discussion of Socrates and Socratic dialogue has reminded us that any "openness to the Other," which we detect as an "ethical condition" of dialogue and understanding, cannot really be called "ethical" unless it is somehow directed toward "the good,"[1] or understood as something valuable for us, either in itself, or in the service of bringing about some ultimate "good." We have also been reminded that interlocutors' willingness to accomplish all the tasks we elaborated as internal to genuine dialogue depends upon a shared notion that such labors are worthwhile and that an understanding of the truths of our world is somehow beneficial to our lives. Socrates, who is constantly trying to cultivate in his interlocutors a care for truth and is always attempting to turn his fellows toward the good, reminds us that we will not be willing to seek truth unless we see it as a desirable, valuable thing. These reminders direct us to the recognition of a second ethical dimension of "play" that has emerged through Gadamer's discussion, which might easily slip by without our noticing, since it is never explicitly stated but is always fully operational — that is, the *value* or *value claim* that engaging in play is ultimately *good for us*. Because some notion of "the good," or "goodness" is essential to any philosophy we want to call "ethical" — and since I am claiming that inherent in Gadamer's philosophical hermeneutics exists an "ethics of play" — it is necessary to point out, if briefly, this implicit value claim.

Gadamer has shown us, as we saw in our discussion of experience (*Erfahrung*) and cultivation (*Bildung*) in chapter 4, that it is only in and through our dialogic "play" with the Other that understanding and self-understanding are made possible, enhanced, and enriched, and we are able to develop beyond the nearsightedness of our own particularity and broaden our horizons. A failure to engage in play, then, results in a lack of learning and a kind of stunted growth. An enriched understanding has even been tied, by Gadamer, to a greater sense of freedom in which we "know our way around" and "feel at home" in matters that previously left

111

us feeling lost, confused, or alienated. Avoiding the difficulties involved in engaging with others and their unfamiliar points of view, and refusing the growing pains involved in expanding or revising our own "comfort zone" of knowledge, result in a limitation of our own possibilities. Furthermore, because "understanding" is considered to be our funda-mental *mode of being* in the world, according to Gadamer (following Heidegger), we see that being a participant in dialogic play with the Other is crucial to what it means to be a human being. As long as dialogic play constitutes, as I have argued, the process of understanding itself, and understanding constitutes our mode of being and developing in the world, we can infer that our continued engagement in play is of the highest ethical significance, since it is only in such play with the Other that we can live, learn, grow, and flourish as human beings.

It is helpful at this point to recall Gadamer's affirmation that "under-standing is the original characteristic of the being of human life itself" and that it is therefore "no longer a methodological concept" (TM, 259). For Gadamer, following Heidegger, hermeneutics takes an ontological turn. For Heidegger, the hermeneutic circle—that process through which one's anticipations of meaning are played out, tried, and revised so that genuine understanding may emerge—is not a methodological circle but "describes an element of the ontological structure of understanding" (TM, 293). All understanding moves in such a circular process in which prejudices are worked out, and our grasp of things is altered, corrected, and enriched. But, insofar as this understanding constitutes our very mode of being and experiencing in the world, the hermeneutic circle describes a fundamental element of our human form of life. Appropriating this insight, Gadamer takes hermeneutics in a universal and ontological direction. Hermeneutics becomes for Gadamer a concern with the entirety of the human being's experiences in the world, and a concern with the very being of the human being itself. Gadamer's phenomenological account of how understanding works becomes an account of *Dasein*: that being who is an *understanding* being-in-the-world, an *interpreting* being-in-the-world, a *dialogical* being-in-the-world and, as I think we are justified in saying at this point in our discussion, a being-*at-play*-in-the-world with others.[2]

The concept of play emerges in Gadamer's work as central to his understanding of what kind of a being the human being is, and what kind of a life the human life is. It is a fundamentally *open* life that is in motion, engaged with others, experiencing, understanding, interpreting, and ap-propriating. The concept of play, as the process of understanding, has helped us to see that the human being is not a subject at a distance from the objects of the world, not a thinking mind distinct from a body, but is a being that is primordially in contact with a world of meaningful things and people, apart from which this being cannot exist. Every moment in which he lives, acts, and finds his way around in his practical existence has the fundamental character of interpretive understanding—an understanding that is enriched through that back-and-forth movement in which he works things out with others and learns something new. He is not a solitary observer, but a participating being-at-play in the ongoing "event" or "game" that is our human form of life.

An important question seems to always arise at this point that is worth addressing. We've been discussing all the commitments and tasks required of interlocutors for genuine dialogic-play and understanding to occur, and we've seen how genuine understanding fails when these commitments are not made. But now we're saying that understanding is *Dasein's* general mode of being. If *Dasein* is always already understanding, then shouldn't understanding continue even when we don't make the commitments to play discussed? The question can be put this way: If understanding is our very mode of being-in-the-world, then don't we still understand even when we don't engage in genuine dialogic-play with the Other? Perhaps my best answer to this, in light of the fact that Gadamer does use "understanding" to refer both to that thing we are always already doing and that thing we are trying so hard to achieve when faced with new meaning, is the following: If you don't make the commitment to engage in play when confronting new meaning (with the "openness to the other" and the "risking of prejudices" involved in that commitment), then you will not build upon your current level of understanding so that you come to "know better." You will remain with your prejudices unrisked, untested, and unplayed. You will remain with your preliminary, parochial "pre-understanding" on the matter, without moving toward an improved or cultivated understanding that always remains a possibility through new genuine engagements with others. Another way to think about this is that there is a difference between a sort of superficial engagement with others and the superficial understanding that results from this, and on the other hand the genuine, rich engagement that brings about genuine, rich understanding. Though we may always be understanding "beings-at-play-in-the-world" with others, we can always enrich our understanding and our way of being in the world. This enrichment is, I take it, one of the primary goals of hermeneutics and is considered an ultimate "good" for our human form of life. When we consider that understanding for Gadamer is both *what* or *who* we already are and, simultaneously, an *achievement* that we want to reach with each other, we can see that the goal of hermeneutic understanding is to be who we are more genuinely, more authentically—to be who we are *better*. I do not know of a goal more ethical in character.

Gadamer's concept of dialogic play is so closely connected to his notion of what it means to be a human being that we are able to recognize that the space of this play is the space of human life—a dynamic, social space of the "in between," in which there exists a joint endeavor to more fully grasp and inhabit a shared world. It is a space that Gadamer's phenomenological reflections guide us to preserve, cultivate, and enrich, and constitutes the ultimate "good" worthy of our care and labors.

NOTES

1. I am not committed to a Platonic notion of the "The Good Itself" that is transcendent and "beyond being" here. The good understood as that which corresponds to a flourishing life will do fine in this discussion.

2. As I mentioned in the introduction, the importance of the concept of play in Gadamer's hermeneutics is usually only recognized in terms of its relevance in its connection with art. Only rarely is it hinted that its relevance stretches to Gadamer's notion of understanding in general, including not only the understanding of artworks, but of texts, history, and the Other in dialogue. I know of only one instance in which it is suggested that play is relevant to understanding Gadamer's vision of our human form of life, or *Dasein* himself. I find this suggestion in Richard Bernstein's analysis of play, where he recognizes the centrality of play for our understanding of dialogue and, because we are dialogical beings, who we are as human beings. He states: "As we explore Gadamer's understanding of philosophical hermeneutics, we will see just how central this concept of play is for him; it turns out to be the key or the clue to his understanding of language and dialogue" (Richard Bernstein, *Beyond Objectivism and Relativism* [Philadelphia: University of Pennsylvania Press, 1983], 121, 122). He, furthermore, argues: "If we are truly dialogical beings—always in conversation, always in the process of understanding—then the dynamics of the play of understanding underlie and pervade all human activities" (Bernstein, *Beyond Objectivism and Relativism*, 137).

Chapter 8

Play and Practical Philosophy: Play as a Guide to Life

In addition to having shown that dialogic play requires necessary ethical conditions, and that the activity of engaged play is of ultimate value to our human form of life, I want to illuminate a third ethical dimension of play, which is revealed in Gadamer's understanding of the intimate connection between theory and practice and the way they endlessly inform each other. Here I want to show that Gadamer's theory of understanding—described as a dynamic, multivocal process—aims *as practical philosophy* to guide our dialogical endeavors to grasp the truths of our world, and to enrich our lives in general. In other words, Gadamer's account of the phenomenon of understanding in terms of play, and his laborious efforts to show all the conditions (including the ethical conditions discussed) which make its genuine movement possible, is ultimately a *guide for praxis*. Implicit in Gadamer's philosophical hermeneutics, then, is an "ethics of play" in a third, distinctly Aristotelian sense—in the sense of an ethical philosophy that offers a guide to a kind of praxis that ultimately enriches our lives in general.

Now, at first glance—and due to remarks Gadamer makes in *Truth and Method* in an effort to distinguish his own work from an earlier tradition of hermeneutics—it might appear that Gadamer's project is not an ethical one at all. Gadamer emphasizes that his undertaking is *philosophical* in nature. What he wants to do, he states explicitly, is to take a good look at the phenomenon of understanding and find out what it really is, what makes it possible, and what happens to us when understanding occurs. He states that he does not intend to give us a technique or method for how to understand, as traditional literary and theological hermeneutics sought to do. He is not writing a "how-to" book. He declares:

> I did not intend to produce a manual for guiding understanding in the manner of the earlier hermeneutics. . . . My real concern was and is

philosophic: not what we do or what we ought to do, but what happens to us over and above our wanting and doing. (TM, xxviii)

He is clear that he is not in the business of formulating a specific set of "prescriptions" or "rules" to follow in order to understand properly, as we might have found in the tradition of literary hermeneutics. Nor does he aim to offer a set of moral rules we must abide by in order to live well, which is perhaps the kind of thing we have come to expect from an ethical treatise. But, although Gadamer insists "it is not my intention to make prescriptions for the sciences or the conduct of life, but to try to correct false thinking about what they are" (TM, xxiii), we should not be misled into thinking Gadamer has no ethical concerns, or even that ethics is not central to his project. Rather, we need to be sensitive to the mode in which Gadamer thinks "the ethical." This is a mode that does not declare absolute ethical rules. It is a mode, rather, that is deeply Aristotelian in character and grounded in a description of the observed practices that promote and preserve human flourishing, and those that hinder it.

THE STAKES OF AN ACCURATE ACCOUNT OF UNDERSTANDING

Gadamer shows us time and again throughout his *Truth and Method* what is really at stake in his project of developing a proper understanding of understanding, and why it is so important to develop better, more accurate conceptions of knowledge and truth. He does this by continually presenting us with instances in which *mis*conceptions and *mis*understandings about what understanding is, how understanding works, and, generally, what makes understanding possible, lead to practices which neglect, ignore, or even silence the voice of the Other who speaks to us (through art, text, tradition, and in living dialogue). These practices, Gadamer shows us, block the possibility of achieving genuine understanding. Misconceptions of what understanding is lead to problematic practices that hinder the development of real understanding and stunt the kind of human growth that occurs in it.

As we have seen (and discussed in chapter 1), the human sciences of the nineteenth century, under the heavy influence of modern science and its conceptions of knowledge and truth, had come to imitate the abstraction procedures involved in scientific method. The human sciences did this in an attempt to achieve for themselves the kind of objective knowledge that would make their own studies worthy of the name "science." This led, as Gadamer argued, to the development in the human sciences of a self-misunderstanding—a misunderstanding of how the human sciences' unique (nonmethodological) kind of understanding really comes about. But, furthermore, the notion that all knowledge is achieved only by following the strict rules of abstraction involved in scientific method, and the detachment of the subject from the meaningful world in which he makes sense of things, also informed strange practices which ultimately served to remove the human scientist from the kind of true engagement that is necessary for truth and understanding to emerge.

Gadamer observed that when "understanding an artwork" is conceived in terms of "aesthetic consciousness," and one is lead to the utilization of the procedures of aesthetic differentiation and the "pure seeing" involved in it, the real being of the artwork itself is destroyed. He says that the effort of "abstracting down to the purely aesthetic obviously eliminates it" (TM, 89). The attempt to ignore a work's context, content, function,and so on, means denying the meaning and the "truth" it tries to present to us. What is suggested, here, is that the effort to engage in such a "pure seeing" of the work of art actually silences the voice of the Other who tries to communicate something through the artwork and results in a kind of violence on the artwork itself. The claim to truth of the Other, here, is given no recognition. Abstracting the very resources that make the work accessible and significant prevents us from undergoing an experience (*Erfahrung*) with it in which we might learn something and share in its truth.

Likewise, Gadamer observed that if we begin with the conception that the meaning of a work of art lies in the author's intention, and attempt to grasp his expressions by way of psychological interpretation, we are lead to another kind of practice that removes us from the kind of real engagement with the work that would allow us to genuinely grasp it. Gadamer says of this approach to the work of art: "To investigate the origin of the plot on which it is based is to move out of the real experience of a piece of literature, and likewise it is to move out of the real experience of the play if the spectator reflects about the conception behind a performance" (TM, 117). The psychological conception of understanding keeps us at a distance from the meaning we need to engage, because it makes us see this meaning as merely the attitude or state of mind of the author, and not a possible truth to be examined that might affect our own thinking.

Finally, Gadamer observed that if we begin in the field of history with a notion that history is a "thing" that may be understood as a whole through a kind of impartiality that requires forgetting ourselves and our own historical situation, we are led down a road where a genuine understanding of history and self-understanding, again, cannot be achieved. Of this notion he states:

> We must here appeal from a badly understood historical thinking to one that can better perform the task of understanding. Real historical thinking must take account of its own historicity. Only then will it cease to chase the phantom of a historical object that is the object of progressive research, and learn to view the object as the counterpart of itself and hence understand both. . . . When naïve faith in scientific method denies the existence of

effective history, there can be an actual deformation of knowledge. (TM, 229, 301)

In bringing to light what genuine understanding is in his hermeneutic theory, Gadamer aims to avoid the kinds of practices that lead to a "deformation of knowledge" and to help us overcome those hurdles to understanding that we've set for ourselves due to our "naïve faith in method." Furthermore, as far as understanding is our very mode of being and developing in the world, Gadamer's hermeneutic theory aims to inform our practices so that we may *live* better.

UNDERSTANDING AND APPLICATION

The fact that Gadamer's hermeneutic theory is meant to inform our practice of understanding — a practice that stretches to every corner of our human form of life and constitutes our very mode of being and developing in the world — becomes clearest when, after having written *Truth and Method*, Gadamer speaks of hermeneutics *as practical philosophy* in the Aristotelian tradition. In his 1976 article "Hermeneutics as Practical Philosophy" Gadamer states: "The great tradition of practical philosophy lives on in a hermeneutics that becomes aware of its philosophic implications. . . . In both cases we have the same mutual implication between theoretical interest and practical action."[1] In this essay, Gadamer establishes explicitly the connection between hermeneutics and ethics by telling us that what ultimately distinguishes practical philosophy from technical knowledge "is that it expressly asks the question of the good,"[2] and that this "holds true for hermeneutics as well" which is not a form of *techne*. Not only is Gadamer's hermeneutics intimately wrapped up with the question of the good, it aims to lead us in a *particular* direction which is conceived by Gadamer to be good for us. On this matter Gadamer, in his 1975 article "Hermeneutics and Social Science," states that the chief task of philosophy is to

> defend practical and political reason against the domination of technology based on science. This is the point of philosophical hermeneutics. It corrects the peculiar falsehood of modern consciousness: the idolatry of scientific method and of the anonymous authority of the sciences and it vindicates again the noblest task of the citizen — decision making according to one's own responsibility — instead of conceding that task to the expert. In this respect, hermeneutic philosophy is the heir of the older tradition of practical philosophy.[3]

Finally, in a 1986 interview, Gadamer expresses the practical lesson of his hermeneutics and the kind of future to which it points in the following way:

What is at issue here is that when something other or different is understood, then we must also concede something, yield—in certain limits—to the truth of the other. That is the essence, the soul of my hermeneutics: To understand someone else is to see the justice, the truth, of their position. And this is what transforms us. And if we then have to become part of a new world civilization, if this is our task, then we shall need a philosophy which is similar to my hermeneutics, a philosophy which teaches us to see the justification for the other's point of view and which thus makes us doubt our own.[4]

Because of these more explicit comments after the publishing of his *Truth and Method* regarding its ethical-practical relevance, some commentators believe that it is only in his later works that he makes a real shift to thinking about ethics. Bernasconi suggests, for instance, that only "late in the day" does Gadamer see his hermeneutic theory as "an ethical demand," and that his late interpretations of his work are inconsistent with what is actually expressed in *Truth and Method*.[5] In opposition to this view, I want to show that these late reflections by Gadamer secure even more tightly the ethical dimensions of his hermeneutics that are *already present* in his *Truth and Method*.

Gadamer's post–*Truth and Method* statements linking his hermeneutics to practical philosophy and ethics are the explicit articulation of something we have seen unfolding all along throughout *Truth and Method*. We can see this, first of all, in Gadamer's emphasis in *Truth and Method* on application. Gadamer goes to great lengths to show that all understanding involves not only interpretation, but also *application*. We remember his assertion that "understanding always involves something like applying the text to be understood to the interpreter's present situation" (TM, 308). Gadamer argues that the fact that all understanding involves application is something the history of hermeneutics teaches us well, which began not only with literary hermeneutics, but also theological and legal hermeneutics. In theological and legal hermeneutics it was clearly understood that the ability to grasp a law (whether it be the law of God, or the law of the state) could not be separated from the ability to apply that law to the concrete situation. As Gadamer argues:

> A law does not exist in order to be understood historically, but to be concretized in its legal validity by being interpreted. Similarly, the gospel does not exist in order to be understood as a merely historical document, but to be taken in such a way that it exercises its saving effect. This implies that the text, whether law or gospel, if it is to be understood properly—i.e., according to the claim it makes—must be understood at every moment, in every concrete situation, in a new and different way. Understanding here is always application. (TM, 309)

Now, this point about the relationship between the law's meaningfulness and its application is a bit more complex than this. It is not as if we first know the meaning of the law on its own before we apply it to a concrete situation. It is not as if the law simply informs its application in a one- way relationship. Gadamer emphasizes that the law itself finds its distinction, significance, and in fact its *existence* only in its application to the concrete situation. The existence of the law and its application, then, are not two separate moments. The law finds its clarification in its concretization, and truly lives only in its application. Rule and case, here, inform each other and enjoy a two-way relationship. In its application to concrete cases, the rule itself is shaped, determined, defined and clarified. Gadamer argues:

> Our knowledge of law and morality too is always supplemented by the individual case, even productively determined by it. The judge not only applies the law in concreto, but contributes through his very judgment to developing the law . . . judging the case involves not merely applying the universal principle according to which it is judged, but co-determining, supplementing, and correcting that principle. (TM, 38–39)

This is the case not just with a legal text, but with any text. Every text, as Gadamer has already shown, aims to make some *claim to truth* about our world, which can only truly be understood and communicated if we are able to grasp how such a truth is applicable to our concrete situation, and how it might lay its claim *upon us*, upon *our* world, upon *our* lives. The truth of any articulation emerges in its applicability to our situation, and we only truly understand such a truth when we apply it in the concreteness of our lives.

Knowledge of such a truth, Gadamer emphasizes, is a very different kind of knowledge from the kind we find in the natural sciences which is used to predict, control, manipulate, or "master phenomena." The knowledge we have been discussing is not "knowledge as domination" but, rather, it is knowledge as openness, receptivity, and service to something greater than ourselves. Again, we must emphasize that, just because the truth or the law that we understand might be spoken and articulated by some other human being, or by "the Other," this does not mean that in understanding and applying what this Other says we are somehow submitting to *his* opinion or serving *him*. The truth which another person articulates is not *his* or *hers*—it is *ours*, or it is not justified in being called truth. When we understand what another person says, we are not agreeing with his or her opinion, we are recognizing the truth in what he or she says. In relation to the truth spoken through tradition, Gadamer states: "The miracle of understanding consists in the fact that no like-mindedness is necessary to recognize what is really significant and fundamentally meaningful in tradition" (TM, 311)—that is, tradition of all kinds, including art, text, and so on. In serving the truth which is spoken by another, through tradition or in living dialogue, we are not bowing down to the other person and allowing him or her to dominate us; we are, rather, bowing to a truth that binds us both, and serving a truth or a law that we must both obey. Understanding has to do with "the ability to open ourselves to the superior claim the text makes and to respond to what it has to tell us" and hermeneutics "consists in subordinating ourselves to the text's claim to dominate our minds" (TM, 311). It is true that all openness and subordination to truth involves an openness to the other person, to whom we must be willing to listen, and to whom we must offer our attention. But *what* we understand, *what* we agree with when we understand, and *what* we ultimately serve is *not the other person* but the truth of what he says. It is in appropriating this truth and critically applying it to our concrete situation that we come to genuinely grasp a truth about our world.

ARISTOTLE AND PRACTICAL KNOWLEDGE

In Gadamer's discussion of the way in which understanding always involves both interpretation *and application*, he has been preparing us to recognize the way in which the knowledge that occurs in the human sciences, and in the totality of our experiences of the world in general, is much closer to what Aristotle calls "practical wisdom" (*phronesis*), than to the methodological knowledge of modern science. Gadamer points out that Aristotle, in his *Nicomachean Ethics*, "is concerned with reason and with knowledge, not detached from a being that is becoming," and asks the question of what is good in terms of human action. "Moral knowledge, as Aristotle describes it, is clearly not objective knowledge—i.e., the knower is not standing over against a situation that he merely observes; he is directly confronted with what he sees. It is something that he has to do" (TM, 312, 314). But the same is the case with the hermeneutic phenomenon—with the phenomenon of understanding the meaning or the claim to truth articulated by some Thou. It is also a situation in which one always already lives, and in which one always has to interpret, try to understand, and act. He says:

> The hermeneutical problem too is clearly distinct from "pure knowledge" detached from any particular kind of being. . . . The human sciences stand closer to moral knowledge than to that kind of "theoretical" knowledge. They are "moral sciences." Their object is man and what he knows about himself. But he knows himself to be an acting being, and this kind of knowledge of himself does not seek to establish what is. An active being, rather, is concerned with what is not always the same but can also be different. In it he can discover the point at which he has to act. The purpose of his knowledge is to govern his *action*. (TM, 314)

To see how Gadamer envisions the hermeneutic phenomenon of understanding as being closely connected to moral knowledge, we must take a closer look at Aristotle's *Nicomachean Ethics* and recognize its relevance for the hermeneutic problem with which Gadamer is concerned.

Aristotle, when he turns to his discussion of the rational part of the soul and its intellectual virtues in Book VI, makes an important distinction between the "scientific part," which deals with theoretical thought, and the "deliberative" part, which deals with practical thought.[6] The scientific-theoretical part apprehends unvarying eternal principles that exist by necessity and cannot be other than they are, regardless of the circumstances. Of this scientific-theoretical part there are three intellectual virtues: *episteme*, *nous*, and *sophia*. *Episteme*, often translated as "pure science" or "pure knowledge" is a knowledge of eternal truths or universal principles, which can be demonstrated, and thus, learned through teaching (e.g., the sum of the three angles of a triangle is 180°). *Nous*, often translated as "intelligence," is a knowledge of the indemonstrable, first principles that constitute the premises from which scientific knowledge is derived (e.g., what an angle is). *Sophia*, often translated as "theoretical wisdom," is a combination of *episteme* and *nous*, and is a knowledge of both fundamental, first principles and what follows from them through demonstration. The purpose of the knowledge acquired by the scientific-theoretical part is "knowledge for its own sake." Though Aristotle calls it the highest kind of knowledge, because it is knowledge of the highest objects—the necessary, eternal, immutable ones—he also considers it to be "useless" because it is a kind of knowledge that gives no direction with regard to how to act.[7] Luckily, we have practical thought for that, and Aristotle distinguishes between two kinds of intellectual virtue achievable by the deliberative or practical part of the soul: *techne* and *phronesis*. Practical thought, unlike theoretical thought, investigates varying, contingent principles whose truth or falsity, rightness or wrongness, are dependent on the particular concrete situation. Practical principles are the principles of right and wrong production (on the one hand) and action (on the other). Whereas the objects with which theoretical thought deals are unchanging things that do not depend on us for their existence, the production and action which practical thought contemplates are distinctively human and brought into being by us—by our making and doing. *Techne*, translated as "art" or "technical knowledge," is a practical knowledge of how to *produce* or make something under the guidance of reason, while *phronesis*, or "practical wisdom," is a knowledge of how to *act* in a way that realizes some good aim. It is an ability to deliberate well with regard to the proper means of action needed in order to attain a good end in each unique circumstance. What Aristotle wants to strengthen in his ethical inquiry is this practical knowledge that will guide us in our action and that will help us to become good.[8]

That ethical knowledge is practical knowledge is an important point for Aristotle, because he feels that he must correct the mistake of equating virtue with *theoretical* knowledge, which is a mistake he finds in Plato's dialogues. Aristotle criticizes Plato's obsession with a metaphysical "Good in itself," above and beyond all particular goods, and asserts that a kind of theoretical knowledge of some absolute and abstract idea of "the Good" will not teach us how to decide and bring about what is good in the particular, concrete situations with which we are always dealing, and in which we must act. To make his point, he makes an analogy early on in Book II:

> One might . . . wonder what benefit a weaver or a carpenter might derive in the practice of his own art from a knowledge of the absolute Good, or in what way a physician who has contemplated the Form of the Good will become more of a physician or a general more of a general. For actually, a physician does not even examine health in this fashion; he examines the health of a man, or perhaps better, the health of a particular man, for he practices his medicine on particular cases. So much for this.[9]

What Aristotle is getting at here is that the good we are seeking is a human good achievable through practice, not a superhuman, eternal Good that is "beyond being." Aristotle insists that we do not just want to know what the good is for its own sake, but we want to know *how to act* and *how to become good* ourselves. Grasping some eternal "Good in Itself" (if such a thing even exists) with theoretical reason will simply not produce this kind of knowledge. Of this sort of theoretical contemplation for its own sake, Aristotle says: "Thought alone moves nothing; only thought which is directed to some end and concerned with action can do so."[10] Practical knowledge is what we need for the task of becoming good ourselves. On this issue, Gadamer interprets Aristotle as holding that "knowledge that cannot be applied to the concrete situation remains meaningless" (TM, 313) and furthermore, it "even risks obscuring what the situation calls for" (TM, 313). Here we see again that the way in which we conceive of knowledge affects, for better or for worse, how we see what a situation calls for and how we respond to it. It, therefore, can have a real moral relevance in its direction or misdirection of our actions.

Aristotle makes clear that ethical knowledge will not be a kind of theoretical knowledge (*episteme*) of eternal laws or facts, not a "knowledge for knowledge's sake" not a kind of "know-that," but, rather, a practical "know-how" that helps us determine how to act in concrete situations. Now, Aristotle warns us, because every situation is different and, thus, demands a different action, the ethical knowledge that we develop through our inquiry will not reach the level of exactitude we attain in our theoretical studies of mathematics, physics and metaphysics, which deal with objects that are immutable and unchanging. Our ethical knowledge will not take the form of precise rules or principles for how to act, but will, rather, take the form of an outline or sketch,[11] drawn from a multitude of concrete examples of human practices, which we will then have to learn how to apply to the individual situations in which we find ourselves. This means that practical knowledge—unlike theoretical knowledge that can be taught through demonstration—will be something that does not follow a strict method and will have to be acquired through time and experience. The ability to sense in general what constitutes better or worse action from a vast variety of unique examples, and the ability to judge the facts of a particular circumstance with which one is dealing in order to determine what is the appropriate action in relation to it, is a knowledge that must be cultivated through observation and practice. Aristotle states:

> An indication that what we have said is correct is the following common observation. While young men do indeed become good geometricians and mathematicians and attain theoretical wisdom in such matters, they apparently do not attain practical wisdom. The reason is that practical wisdom is concerned with particulars as well *as with universals*, and knowledge of particulars comes from experience. But a young man has no experience, for experience is the product of a long time. In fact, one might also raise the question why it is that a boy may become a mathematician but not a philosopher or a natural scientist. The answer may be that the objects of mathematics are the result of abstraction, whereas the fundamental principles of philosophy and natural science come from experience. Young men can assert philosophical and scientific principles but can have no genuine convictions about them, whereas there is no obscurity about the essential definitions in mathematics. [12]

From such time and experience, Aristotle detects that "the nature of moral qualities is such that they are destroyed by defect and by excess" [13] and— as an outline of the phenomena before him—suggests that virtue is preserved by "the mean."

Through numerous examples of human behavior, Aristotle attempts to draw a sketch of what this "mean" might be in all our various types of behavior, developing a list of moral virtues that fall at a moderate middle ground between excess and defect. But, it is still *up to us* to decipher through *deliberation* what particular course of action is called for in each concrete situation that will promote and preserve virtue in each individual case, and it is also up to us to *act* accordingly by our free choice (*proairesis*). The ability to do all this well, and to cultivate excellence (*arete*) in practical matters, requires a harmony of practical wisdom and moral virtue, which takes practice and habits of action. For this reason, Aristotle's sketch of moral principles can act only as a kind of arrow that points us in the general direction of where we ought to aim with our actions; but it is a crucial guideline that we cannot do without if we are to develop virtue. As Gadamer puts it, "in moral knowledge . . . it is clear that experience can never be sufficient for making right moral decisions . . . moral consciousness itself calls for prior direction to guide action" (TM, 316). Aristotle, "by outlining phenomena, helps moral consciousness to attain clarity concerning itself" (TM, 313). [14] Action needs practical knowledge to govern it and point it in the right direction. This is the value of an ethical philosophy.

APPLYING GADAMER'S PHILOSOPHICAL HERMENEUTICS

Just as Aristotle's ethical philosophy is generated out of an observation of the phenomena of human action that he experiences—phenomena in which we always already take part as human actors—Gadamer's hermeneutic philosophy of understanding is generated out of a phenomenological analysis of practices of understanding and of interpreting meaning in which we are also always already engaged as human beings. From Aristotle we learn that the nature of the subject matter of practical reasoning determines the fact that any principles, rules, or truths we will be able to formulate for ourselves, with regard to the kind of action that is ultimately good for us, will be suggestive guidelines requiring interpretation and judgment in each of its applications. Any practical knowledge we come to, by looking at a variety of examples of human life in action, will still require concretization in the particular case with which we are confronted. The same is the case for hermeneutics, for the understanding and interpretation of any meaning always involves application.

This is a relevant insight for the way in which *we* understand Gadamer's philosophical hermeneutics as laid out in his *Truth and Method*—for here too we are presented with meaning we are trying to grasp, and so must interpret and apply. Here too we are presented with some outline of phenomena, some account of the way things are for us, some philosophy—this time with regard to the way understanding works. Just like Aristotle's sketch of how virtue is cultivated, this philosophy has been drawn from concrete experiences or practices—in this case practices of interpretation and instances in which the phenomenon of understanding has occurred. Here too, we are offered a philosophy regarding our practices, which will find its full meaning and truth in our application of its truth back in our own practices. Gadamer states: "Application does not mean first understanding a given universal in itself and then afterward applying it to a concrete case. It is the very understanding of the universal—the text—itself. Understanding proves to be a kind of effect and knows itself as such" (TM, 341). Our understanding—in general, and in the particular case of grasping Gadamer's hermeneutics—thus becomes fully concretized in the effect it has upon us in our enactment, performance, and application of it.[15]

Just as Aristotle's sketch of the kind of action that cultivates virtue is meant to be put into practice by us if it is going to have any value at all, Gadamer's phenomenological analysis of the workings of understanding, and his efforts to correct the widespread misunderstandings about it that have developed from the dominating model of scientific method, has its value also as a guide to our own practical efforts to understand. But, just like Aristotle's ethics, Gadamer's hermeneutics cannot be reduced to a kind of technical knowledge to be utilized in some "art of understanding." It is not a *techne*, which is, I take it, what Gadamer was trying to emphasize when he declared that he was not attempting to lay down a set of rules for understanding. Nor is it a type of theoretical knowledge (*episteme*) of eternal laws that can be grasped through some sort of demonstration, which, I take it, he was trying to emphasize when he declared that he was not going to lay down a set of rules for our conduct. It is rather a sketch of guidelines, developed out of an analysis of practices in which understanding has occurred, which can direct and improve our future practices. Philosophical hermeneutics must be conceived as a practical philosophy.

Just like the "action" with which Aristotle was concerned, understanding is something that penetrates our human form of life completely. Any concern, then, with what makes it possible, what makes it work, and what makes it go right in the most genuine of ways in which we undergo a truly enriching transformation is a concern with what is of the utmost ethical significance; it is a concern with what makes possible an enriched human life in general. Gadamer's concern with genuine understanding and his account of it in terms of dialogic play, along with his discussion of all the conditions that make that movement of play possible, emerge not only as a hermeneutic philosophy, but as an ethical philosophy as well.

NOTES

1. Hans-Georg Gadamer, "Hermeneutics as Practical Philosophy," in *Reason in the Age of Science*, trans. Frederick G. Lawrence (Cambridge: MIT Press, 1981), 111.
2. Gadamer, "Hermeneutics as Practical Philosophy," 93.
3. Hans-Georg Gadamer, "Hermeneutics and Social Science," in *Cultural Hermeneutics* 2, no. 1 (May 1974): 316.
4. Dieter Misgeld and Graeme Nicholson, eds., *Hans-Georg Gadamer on Education, Poetry, and History: Applied Hermeneutics* (Albany: SUNY Press, 1992), 152.
5. Robert Bernasconi, "'You Don't Know What I'm Talking About': Alterity and the Hermeneutic Ideal," in *The Specter of Relativism*, ed. Lawrence Schmidt (Evanston, Ill.: Northwestern University Press, 1995), 179, 191.
6. In our discussion of Aristotle we will use the term "theoretical" in the strict sense that Aristotle does, which refers to the sort of reasoning that grasps eternal laws. Elsewhere it will be more useful to use the term in the wider sense that refers to a philosophical theory of any kind, including types of practical (ethical or hermeneutical) theory.
7. Aristotle, *Nicomachean Ethics*, trans. Martin Ostwald (New York: Macmillan Publishing Company, 1962), 1141b8.
8. I say "strengthen" here because a lecture on ethics will not be enough to fully develop practical wisdom. We will need practice as well. A reflective inquiry into ethics, based on our observations of the practices that promote and destroy virtue, will, though, give us vision and guidance in our practical efforts.
9. Aristotle, *Nicomachean Ethics*, 1097a10.
10. Aristotle, *Nicomachean Ethics*, 1139a36.
11. See Aristotle, *Nicomachean Ethics*, 1094b20, 1104a.

12. Aristotle, *Nicomachean Ethics*, 1142a12.

13. Aristotle, *Nicomachean Ethics*, 1104a12.

14. The rest of this quote follows: "This asks a lot of the person who is to receive this help, namely the person listening to Aristotle's lecture. He must be mature enough not to ask that his instruction provide anything other than it can and may give. To put it positively, through education and practice he must himself already have developed a demeanor that he is constantly concerned to preserve in the concrete situations of his life and prove through right behavior" (TM, 313). This, I take it, is a good example of the kind of ethical conditions for dialogue that were discussed in chapter 5. The student, if he is going to learn anything from Aristotle, and if he is going to enter into a genuine dialogue with him or with his text, must not have to ask why learning general ethical guidelines are worthwhile, or why he should listen to Aristotle at all. He must already be an open and willing listener out of an already ingrained notion that coming to an understanding of such matters are good for him.

15. Gadamer himself simultaneously performs the truth that all understanding involves application while explicitly stating it. What is marvelous about Gadamer's account of understanding as dialogic play is that while he is articulating it and bringing the phenomenon into speech, he is simultaneously enacting the process of dialogic play in deed, for he is in constant dialogue throughout *Truth and Method* with the figures in the history of philosophy who have influenced him. As he *speaks* about understanding tradition as an appropriation of what the Thou says to us across time, and as an application of its truth in relation to our own concerns, we see him *do* this appropriation with Plato, Aristotle, Heidegger, and others. For a man who was so impressed by the Socratic harmony of speech (*logos*) and deed (*ergon*) (see Gadamer's "Logos and Ergon in Plato's Lysis" in *Dialogue and Dialectic: Eight Hermeneutical Studies on Plato*, trans. P. Christopher Smith [New Haven, Conn.: Yale University Press, 1980]), we should hope that Gadamer could recognize that he too achieved such a harmony in his own work. It is worth remarking, also, that inasmuch as we read and understand *Truth and Method*, listen to the claim to truth articulated by Gadamer, and appropriate it in ways that allow it to speak meaningfully to our own philosophical interests and contemporary problems, we too participate in the grand dialogue which constitutes the hermeneutical practice.

Part IV

When Ethical Conditions are Lacking

In part III, I aimed to illuminate the ethical dimensions of Gadamer's philosophical hermeneutics, arguing that implicit in Gadamer's account of understanding is what I called an "ethics of play." By this I meant that we find in Gadamer's phenomenological description of understanding as an "event of play" (1) an articulation of the ethical conditions that make such play possible (namely, interlocutors' openness to each other, their good will to understand each other, and their directedness toward truth as their ultimate goal), (2) the operating value claim that our engaged play with the Other in which understanding occurs is ultimately *good* for us, in that it constitutes and enriches our human form of life, and (3) an account of understanding-as-play that aims, as practical philosophy, to guide our dialogical play-engagements with others in which we might improve our communication and our shared grasp of the world.

Gadamer has shown us throughout his *Truth and Method* what is really at stake in his project of developing an accurate account of understanding, for he has shown us that a proper notion of understanding is needed if our efforts to grasp our world in a more complete and profound way are to be given proper direction. Though understanding constitutes our very mode of being-in-the-world, and we are thus always already understanding, every new experience presents us with the possibility of alienation, confusion, and a rupture in understanding. But this means, for Gadamer, that every new experience also presents us with an opportunity for our understanding to grow, shift, and become deeper. Hermeneutics, as a theory and practice of understanding and correct interpretation, aims to confront the alienation we face with new meaning, and to learn from the Other in what proves to be an open-ended process of grasping the unfolding truths of our shared world. The account of understanding that Gadamer provides aims to give us guidance in our efforts to reach understanding with one another, and works to help us past various obstacles that stand in the way of our quest.

Among the most difficult of these obstacles, for Gadamer, are those derived from a modern scientific project of knowledge, which prescribes practices of objectification that remove us from the participatory play in which genuine communicative understanding occurs. Following such prescriptions, we might (even with the best intentions) try to understand the Other, but believe that this is to be accomplished by encountering the Other as a natural "thing." We might study the human "thing" by watching the Other's patterns of behavior and trying to predict them. Or, in a derivative version of this approach, we might believe that understanding the Other is to be accomplished by making his psyche into our "object" of investigation, and trying to decipher the life experiences and personal viewpoints that his utterances express. Another significant obstacle to understanding that we set for ourselves is the one that results from the sophistic project of attempting to overpower the Other in an argument. In the spirit of such a sophistic project we might listen intently to what the Other says, but only for the purpose of discovering the weakness or "hole" in his argument, believing that this kind of criticism alone is the mark of intelligence. These three projects have gained an overwhelmingly dominant place in our society, finding their expression not only in the disciplines of the natural and social sciences, technology, politics, and law, but also in the popular consciousness and contemporary common sense that draws its inspiration from them. From Gadamer's account of understanding, we learn that we must give up these popular scientific, psychological, and sophistic projects if we are going to remove the obstacles that keep us from a genuine participation with our interlocutor.[1] Instead, we must *open* ourselves to a kind of listening in which we allow our own prejudgments to be truly challenged and transformed. In accounting for the ethical conditions, which make the play of understanding possible, Gadamer is able to give guidance to those who are eager in their efforts to achieve understanding, but who have fallen into a misconception about what understanding really is.

But this is just where we begin to see the limits of Gadamer's account of understanding as a guide to praxis. We find ourselves approaching an edge. Philosophical Hermeneutics *as* practical philosophy aims to guide us in our dialogical encounters with others, yet at the same time reveals to us that any genuine understanding relies on a *shared ethical commitment* and *mutual openness*. Gadamer's phenomenological description of understanding always begins with two interlocutors who *want* to develop understanding and who are *willing* to talk to each other. They may not have a correct notion of what that understanding really is, but they *want* knowledge (in the various ways they conceive of that knowledge) and they are *willing* to speak and be spoken to. They are at least "open" enough for that. But this means that Gadamer's guide past the various roadblocks that we set for ourselves, in our dialogical relations with others, begins where the biggest and most threatening contemporary

obstacle to dialogue and understanding has already been overcome—
namely, the refusal to listen.

NOTES

1. Since the scientific, psychological, and sophistic projects have become so dominant in western culture, Gadamer's warning about them serves as a kind of social
critique.

Chapter 9

The Problem of Closedness

"Could you really persuade if we don't listen?" Polemarchus asks Socrates in the opening lines of Plato's *Republic* (*Republic*, 327c). Here Plato expresses the crux of the problem that we have watched escalate to new heights. We have heard political leaders declare, with regard to international conflict, that "there will be no more negotiations," "no more talk" — that the time for talk is over. We have found growing division between members of polarizing political parties, where dialogue is abandoned. We have found friends and family members say surprising things like: "I can't even talk to someone who voted for . . ." (fill in the blank). We experience a fundamental split in sensibility and in basic values, and sometimes find ourselves believing that any attempt to understand each other is futile. We even begin to develop the sense that we don't even *want* to understand each other . . . because, after all, why would we want to understand people who believe in something so fundamentally opposed to what we hold dear? Positions begin to appear black and white, sides are taken or assigned, and whoever is on "the other side" begins to be characterized as the unintelligible and the alien. This kind of division, which leads to radical communication breakdown, can be observed in everything from international politics, to religious disputes, to racial friction, to the "battle of the sexes," to debates between the so-called camps of analytic and continental philosophy. We also find the phenomenon occurring between parents and children, husbands and wives, employers and employees, landlords and tenants, and in almost every type of law suit, where parties have become so "closed" to dialogue that they find themselves compelled to hire someone else to talk for them in what is inevitably an adversarial nondialogue before a judge or jury. The areas where we overlap, the common issues and interests that give us something to talk about, the frame of reference in which we might begin to understand each other better or develop a transformed and improved grasp of the issues that have become so controversial, is increasingly ignored. It is this culture of division and dialogue abandonment that constitutes our most threatening contemporary barrier to understanding.

There is a level of "closedness" to the Other that Gadamer is able to guide us past in his instructive descriptions of the ethical conditions that make genuine understanding possible. For instance, if we want to communicate and understand each other, and are "open" enough to listen to each other, but we are listening to the wrong thing or listening in the wrong way, Gadamer's account of understanding has the power to guide us from a sort of provisional, superficial dialogue to a deeper engaged play in which our grasp of truth has a chance to develop together. Where interlocutors share a basic ethical comportment toward each other and toward the goal of understanding, but are in need of direction and insight that will allow them to develop their potential, Gadamer's philosophy has the power to aid the cultivation of a richer relationship and understanding. The movement, then, through which Gadamer is able to guide us is the movement from a state of basic friendship (in our shared ethical commitment to understand) to an even better friendship (in a richer common understanding of the subject matter and our common goals). But the problem that we confront, in a society increasingly divided into separate subcultures, and in a world where peoples of vastly different traditions must learn how to become a global community, is to know how to cultivate such an ethical friendship in the first place and become, at the very least, the kind of friends who are *willing to try* to understand each other for the common good. Our biggest problem is how we are to cultivate an openness toward the Other in those people (including ourselves) who have become radically "closed" to the Other, so that we can get the process of "understanding," and the genuine encounter with each other that is internal to it, off the ground. This task that stands before us is one that cannot be fulfilled by drawing on Gadamerian "genuine dialogue" for guidance, because it presupposes the very ethical comportment of openness that we want to develop. We cannot simply persuade someone that understanding is important and that "openness" and a serious acknowledgment of the other's "claim to truth" that understanding requires are worthwhile if they have no desire to listen to us. In this context, Gadamer's philosophical hermeneutics leaves us hanging where we are most in need of direction.

REACHING THE LIMITS OF PHILOSOPHICAL HERMENEUTICS

The experience we have when encountering the limit of Gadamer's hermeneutics, in its ability to act as a guide, recalls that frustration many of us feel in reading the classic text that has had such a deep influence on Gadamer's philosophical hermeneutics—Aristotle's *Nicomachean Ethics.* Aristotle's *Ethics,* as Aristotle recognizes and declares outright, can only act as a guide to those who already understand the importance of ethics and have already been raised in the right way. If a potential student in Aristotle's lecture has to ask why he should try to live ethically, or why living ethically is good, he is not properly prepared for an ethical-political study. One must already accept that virtue is good and desire to achieve it, if a course in ethics is going to speak to one meaningfully and be worthwhile in any way. If Aristotle's audience is not already open to the ethical life, his lecture will fall on deaf ears and will not "pull in" his students in an engaged manner. Its power as a guide, just as we have seen with Gadamer's magnum opus, presupposes an ethical *opening to the good* along with an ethical *opening to the Other* and what he has to say. Yet, at the same time, we find in Aristotle a general optimism that he who has not been raised right is not a "hopeless case," but can—through the right habits of action—inevitably cultivate virtue too. In light of this, we might find ourselves asking: "But how are we supposed to reach that person?" or "What good is an ethics that only reaches people who are already good?" Though I hope that I have answered the second question and showed how those who already find themselves desiring an enriched life of excellence still need the vision and direction to accomplish it (which is what an ethical philosophy aims to provide in some way), the first question still stands.

Taking a step further back in time, we find an even closer resemblance to the limit we have encountered in Gadamer's philosophy—the limit to what we might call the "opening power" of Gadamer's hermeneutics. This limit seems to be the same one that Socrates faced with regard to what he could accomplish in his encounters with others. As mentioned in chapter 6, Socrates' first task was to inspire an opening to dialogue and to truth, and to cultivate that ethical friendship with his interlocutors that was necessary for the upward way of the genuine dialectical dialogue. But, even Socrates' most resistant and contentious interlocutors—even the sophists who Socrates attempted to turn toward genuine dialogue for the good of their souls—were *willing* to talk and listen (even if not yet in a *genuine* way).[1] And even Polemarchus, who threatens to turn a deaf ear to the persuasive power of Socratic *logos*, proves to be merely toying with Socrates; for his true goal is not to deny Socrates dialogue, but to get him to stay in Piraeus precisely for the purpose of a willing conversation. But at no time do we watch Socrates persuade or draw into dialogue a figure unwilling to listen at all. So, what *can* we do when our "Other" or our "Thou" has become so *radically closed* that the effort and "good will" to listen, speak, and understand in the most basic of ways are lacking? What can we do when we reach such an impasse to dialogue? How can we overcome this limit?

Despite the defenses that I have offered for Gadamer's philosophical hermeneutics in the face of the various limits for which it is criticized, I too want to bring attention to a limit. In fact, I too am concerned with the problem of difference, though a very specific difference that I do not believe is untouchable in principle, but is surely untouched within the hermeneutical process described by Gadamer. My concern regarding the limit of difference is specifically the concern of whether or not Gadamer's hermeneutics is able to act as a guide for us when we are faced with the particular difference we meet in the person unwilling to engage in dialogue. This difference can be characterized as a basic "ethical difference" that manifests itself as a comportment of "closedness" to the Other, to the activity of dialogue, and to the value of such a dialogue in which a shared understanding can develop. The particular ethical difference that constitutes the limit to which I want to call attention, then, *is not* the sort of difference in ethical position that might emerge between us *in and through an ethical debate* (e.g., over whether or not the good life is achieved through pleasure, honor, money, or wisdom; or over whether we have a responsibility to protect the rights of an unborn fetus; or over whether it is acceptable to use physical force to elicit information from prisoners of war). There is plenty of room in Gadamer's account of dialogue for these different ethical points of view to play themselves out and emerge in conversation. The ethical difference I mean to point out as a limit is a much more fundamental and basic ethical disjunction that makes it impossible for such a debate to even get started. Any meaningful and substantial opposition we might encounter from the Other with regard to specific moral problems cannot even find articulation until this first, fundamental difference in ethical comportment is overcome. Though I believe that Gadamer is able to accommodate the differences in perspective we find between I and Thou that emerge *in dialogue*, differences that I've called the "lifeblood" of dialogic play, there is a very specific difference that Gadamer cannot accommodate in his account of understanding—the radical closedness to the Other and refusal to engage in dialogue in the first place. Gadamer *is not* able to accommodate difference on this very basic ethical level, because his theory of genuine understanding depends wholly on interlocutors sharing a common *value* in understanding and a mutual ethical *commitment* to strive for this understanding in the most effective way. Without a mutual willingness to engage openly with the Other, there can be no dialogue-play and no genuine understanding.

THE SPACE OF PLAY AND THE SPACE OF LIFE: THE NEED FOR ALTERNATIVES TO DISENGAGEMENT AND FORCE

In the face of this particular limit situation—where we encounter radical closedness and a refusal to engage in dialogue—we are often struck with a sense of paralysis that might lead us to completely disengage, retreat, or withdraw from any kind of encounter with the Other. Walls go up, camps become segregated, and a kind of isolationism sets in. Alternatively, there might be a turn to force, where an attempt is made to simply overpower the Other (a disturbingly popular choice). But when we consider, as Gadamer has shown us, that our very mode of being and developing in the world depends upon our continued to-and-fro engagement with the Other, we see that our involvement in dialogue-play with those different from ourselves is crucial to our very form of life. Disengagement from the Other, the complete restriction of the Other's participation, the elimination of the Other—or any other "game-stopping" moves—constitute the worst kind of violence to our human form of life. In fact, if we remember Gadamer's use of the term play in its broadest sense, we can see that disengagement and force actually constitute a violence to the movement of *life* in general.

Play, as I have argued, is a crucial concept for understanding the structure of understanding and our unique *human* form of life. But, returning to the concept of play in its broadest sense, it is a crucial concept for understanding *life* at large. Early on in chapter 3, with the introduction of the concept of play, we saw briefly that play is a natural process and that the human being, as far as he is a part of nature, also plays. In his essay "The Play of Art," Gadamer states: "Play is an elementary phenomenon that pervades the whole of the animal world and, as is obvious, it determines man as a natural being as well."[2] Our turn to the distinctiveness of *human* play—which has both ethical and linguistic dimensions—was made almost immediately in our discussion. But, when Gadamer says "play," what he means first and foremost is a certain freedom of *movement* or (more properly) self-movement. And this is just the movement, following Aristotle, that is inherent in anything that lives. In "The Relevance of the Beautiful," Gadamer states:

> Expressing the thoughts of the Greeks in general, Aristotle had already described self-movement as the most fundamental characteristic of living beings. Whatever is alive has its source of movement within itself and has the form of self-movement. Now play appears as a self-movement that does not pursue any particular end or purpose so much as movement *as* movement, exhibiting so to speak a phenomenon of excess, of living self-representation. And in fact that is just what we perceive in nature. . . . All this arises from the basic character of excess striving to express itself in the living being.[3]

Here we begin to see more fully how our distinctively human dialogic play, through which we communicate with each other and strive together to articulate and understand the meaningful truths of our world and ourselves, is rooted in the natural movement of life to show itself or to present itself. (We recall that Gadamer calls "self-presentation" the very mode of being of play.) The space of play, then, is something ultimately broader than the space of dialogue. Dialogue is a distinctively human form of play—one peculiar manifestation of a movement that stretches beyond human language, human understanding, and human life, and connects us with the rest of nature. Gadamer urges us in "The Play of Art" to recognize the "universal scope and ontological dignity of play" and to see it as the "vital ground of spirit as nature, a form of restraint and freedom at one and the same time."[4] Gadamer urges us, I believe, to recognize that the space of play is the space of life—a space that is up to us (we, whose practice [*praxis*] is directed by choice [*proairesis*]) to preserve.[5] When we encounter a refusal or closedness to engage in the play of dialogue—that play that is so central to our distinctively human form of life—we must, then, find other modes of engagement, other modes of play that can reopen the possibility of dialogue, and provide an alternative to the options of withdrawal and force that halt dialogue-play and, furthermore, destroy the back-and-forth movement that is essential to all that is living.

Though Gadamer's hermeneutics, as I have argued, offers us guidance in our engagements with others who are open to us in the basic manner necessary for dialogue to get started, and though Gadamer's hermeneutics helps us to move from a sort of superficial friendship to a deeper one of genuine understanding, we surely recognize that it is not just when we are faced with our other "friends" that we need a practical philosophy or ethics that will guide us to a more genuine encounter with the Other. We also need guidance when faced with a more radical Other who does not share the desire to engage in dialogue, or the good will to understand us. What must be avoided at the moment that dialogue is rejected is the rejection of engagement altogether, for the turn to disengagement or force is ultimately destructive of the play-movement central to life. What is needed is a broader "ethics of play" that can guide us in our relations with others where dialogue has been rejected or has disintegrated, and that can help us to bring about an opening or re-opening to dialogue.

NOTES

1. Even Thrasymachus, who Socrates ultimately has to "tame" in order to get a genuine dialogue started, is just a sophist and not a so-called barbarian with whom one cannot speak (in multiple senses—not only because a barbarian does not speak Greek, but also because his approach is usually one of physical force).

2. Hans-Georg Gadamer, "The Play of Art," in *The Relevance of the Beautiful*, ed. Robert Bernasconi (Cambridge: Cambridge University Press, 1986), 123.

3. Hans-Georg Gadamer, "The Relevance of the Beautiful," in *The Relevance of the Beautiful*, ed. Robert Bernasconi (Cambridge: Cambridge University Press, 1986), 23.

4. Gadamer, "The Play of Art," 130.

5. There are resources here for an ethics that stretches to include our relationship with nonhuman forms of life (i.e., an "environmental ethics").

Chapter 10

Cultivating an Opening to Dialogue

It is just when we are faced with an unwillingness to engage in dialogue that we must find alternatives to totally disengaging from the Other, or overpowering the Other with force. We must find new forms of participation with the Other in which we can keep the movement central to life going, and which might cultivate an opening to the dialogical process that constitutes our mode of being and developing in the world. In the face of an impasse to dialogue, we must find new forms of *play*—the game must go on. As a last task of this work, I want to begin to consider how we might cultivate such an opening to dialogue by drawing on the notion of play in its broadest sense—a sense that includes modes of dynamic engagement with the Other beyond explicit conversation. This last task will involve the work of thinking with Gadamer in order to continue the conversation begun by him and to reach beyond the limits of the practical philosophy that has guided us this far.

In search of resources from Gadamer's philosophy that would help us to face the impasse to dialogue, which has become an increasingly serious problem in our era, we can begin with the observation that though an individual might be closed in one way—in this case, to dialogue in certain situations, or with certain people—it is unlikely, and perhaps impossible, for one to be fundamentally "closed" in all ways. If we are, as Gadamer has suggested, fundamentally dialogical beings, then there is a sense in which we are fundamentally "open" beings by nature. We could not "be-in-the-world" without having a primordial character of openness that allows us to interact with things and people, find our way around, experience, learn, and speak. This, I think, makes good sense whether we are working with a Heideggerian sensibility, or whether we have just had the common experience of watching small children learn, grow, "find" things in their world for the first time, start to say the words that they hear from their parents, and ask for things. None of this could take place unless there were, in these young human beings, a sort of natural openness to the world in which they find themselves, to the meaningful things and people that stand in relation to them, and to the voices of others. An individual might learn to close herself off in certain situations, and create for herself a kind of obstacle to growth and learning. But this "closedness" represents a sort of self-inflicted block to one's own potential and possibility, and even a break in what might otherwise be a more natural course of development. Though one might learn to be "closed" in one way, this doesn't mean that she will be closed in all ways—for that would, likely, lead to a kind of life that we would barely recognize as human. In the event of what I have termed a "closedness" to dialogue, we must look for other openings, or a willingness to engage in other kinds of interaction—other kinds of games—that can lead to an opening to conversation.

LANGUAGE AND THE WORD

Now, we might hear a good Gadamerian object that *all* our human games are at bottom dialogical, so that we will find no nondialogical games toward which we humans can turn. After all, he might say, that is what it means to be a dialogical being! This objection needs to be addressed before we can legitimately search for nondialogical games that might open us to dialogue.

In one way I think we can agree with this good Gadamerian's reply, if we are using the concept of language and dialogue in the broadest sense— in the sense that includes things like gesture, body language, laughing, crying, drawing, singing, dancing, and so forth. Through customary practices like these, there is much that we communicate to each other in a back-and-forth movement, and much that we learn from each other and hand down to our children without stating anything in words. We find such a broad sense in Gadamer's use of the word "language" on numer-ous occasions. After all, he is the one who has considered *all* tradition— including not only written and oral tradition, but also *all* types of art (drama, music, dance, painting, sculpture) and different forms of ritual— to be *language* that must be interpreted and understood. If we use "language" in this broad sense we would say that all our human games are dialogical, though not all explicitly verbal, which would allow us to still seek out nonverbal types of engagement that could lead us to explicit dialogue.

But if, on the other hand, we are using the term "language" in the narrow sense of the verbal "word"—which Gadamer himself begins to do in the third part of *Truth and Method*—then we'd better pause for a moment to recognize that there are all sorts of spaces in our lives, to which Gadamer himself has called attention early on, where we interact in a reciprocal movement of understanding without articulating something explicitly. Even our perception, we recall from chapter 1, is a "seeing-as" and involves interpretation, articulation, and understanding. There is a certain level of understanding, Gadamer had argued, implicit in *all our human experience in the world*. In this case we can still look for nonverbal play-engagements with the Other that might open us to explicit dialogue.

But what of this narrow use of the term "language" that begins to appear in the closing pages of the second part of *Truth and Method*? Is Gadamer not in tension with himself when he begins to make language mean "the word?" Gadamer surely had argued before this point that all understanding has the structure of dialogue and takes place in and through language, and that we, whose mode of being-in-the-world is understanding, are linguistic beings. But now understanding and its linguisticality (*Sprachlichkeit*) begins to be associated with the *explicit word* exclusively. Gadamer states of our understanding of the subject matter that it "must take the form of language. It is not that the understanding is subsequently put into words; rather, the way understanding occurs — whether in the case of a text or a dialogue with another person who raises an issue with us — is the coming-into language of the thing itself" (TM, 378). The transition here is so smooth, that we barely notice the emphasis on the literal "word" and the suggestion that understanding itself cannot be wordless. But this idea is quickly picked up in the opening to part III of *Truth and Method*, where Gadamer declares of the experience (*Erfahrung*) of meaning that takes place in understanding, "*that this whole process is verbal*" (TM, 384). We cannot help but remember that the first time Gadamer mentioned the real experience (*Erfahrung*) of meaning that happens to us when we understand, he was referring to our experience of a work of art, which certainly did not need to be in the form of a "verbal" presentation to an audience and their "verbal" recognition. But now we find Gadamer curiously saying that "the essence of tradition is to exist in the medium of language, so that the preferred *object* of interpretation is a verbal one" (TM, 389). He explains that verbal tradition has special priority over all other kinds of tradition, because it is truly *given* or *handed down* to us and, thus, is tradition in the proper sense of the word. Tradition that has been verbalized is tradition that has been articulated *for us*, has been *told to us* so that it is immediately clear to us, unlike a "dumb" (*stumm*: dumb, mute, speechless) monument, which he says is "simply left over" from the past (TM, 390). (This is a strange choice of words coming from someone so sensitive to the way nonliterary art too *articulates* something to us.)

Now, a reader of the German might notice that the word being translated as verbal is actually "*sprachlich*," whose meaning as "linguistic" would be broad enough to include nonverbal forms of language. But as we read on, we cannot ignore that Gadamer continually emphasizes the "explicit" nature of understanding in which some subject matter is "put into words." He states, for instance: "All understanding is interpretation, and all interpretation takes place in the medium of language that allows the object to come into words" (TM, 389). Language in the sense of "the verbal" is defined, here, not only as the hermeneutic object—or *what* it is that we understand—but, furthermore, as the hermeneutic act. Coming to an understanding occurs in the coming to articulate speech of what we understand. Gadamer states: "Interpretation is . . . the act of understanding itself, which is realized . . . in the explicitness of verbal interpretation" (*in der Ausdrücklichkeit sprachlicher Auslegung*) (TM, 397; WM, 401). It is not as if we first understand, and second give that understanding a voice in verbal interpretation. Language, Gadamer insists, is not a tool we use to communicate something we already knew previously. Rather, it is only through the word that we come to know something at all. He says: "The word is not formed only after the act of knowledge has been completed . . . it is the act of knowledge itself" (TM, 424). Language is so fully the medium of all understanding, that even the movement of thinking is accomplished only with words and is fundamentally the process of bringing the subject matter to explicit language (if silently, as a kind of internal dialogue). Here, understanding and language (in the sense of words) cannot be separated in their being.

But what has happened here to the interpretive understanding I experience in listening to a symphony, or in my own guitar playing, or tennis playing, dancing, drawing—or even in finding my way from the subway to work everyday by way of numerous different routes? Surely these are all activities in which I understand something, *know* my way around, and even communicate with others without being explicitly verbal, or stating my knowledge with words. To this, Gadamer's response is that even "in those cases when there is immediate understanding and no explicit interpretation is undertaken . . . interpretation must be possible" (TM, 398). It might seem as if we have here a contradiction. On the one hand we hear Gadamer telling us that understanding only really occurs when it is articulated verbally; on the other hand, there is something like an implicit, nonverbal kind of understanding that exists as the basic character of our experience and our very mode of being-in-the-world. Perhaps this apparent tension can be overcome if we offer the following suggestion. We are dealing here with a matter of degree in understanding. There is a basic level of understanding involved in our immediate, practical experience in the world, but this implicit understanding is pregnant with potential and possibility—the potential of reaching explicit articulation and, in such a process, becoming clarified, fleshed out, and enriched. But, one should add, it is not as if language in the sense of the explicit word is not at all involved in that more immediate experience in the world described. Gadamer believes that "experience is not wordless" (TM, 417). I may know my way around Greenwich Village without speaking words, but surely things like "the subway," "Washington Square," "14th Street" are all things that were pointed out to me with words and that I learned with the use of explicit language. They became a meaningful part of my world when they began to be spoken to me and I, in turn, began to speak them. The word, as Gadamer likes to put it, shines light on a thing so that it is able to appear, show itself, and become present. My "knowing my way around," in this example and ones like it, then, *presuppose* language—presuppose "the word"—according to Gadamer.

Now we are beginning to see how it is that the human world itself (according to Gadamer) is constituted linguistically in the sense of explicit language. Explicit language is what allows some subject matter to be brought to presentation "as" something, so that it becomes a distinct, meaningful part of our world. Again, language, Gadamer insists, is not just a tool at our disposal that we use to refer to the things in our world— rather, we would not have a world or the things in it at all without language. He states: "Not only is the world world only insofar as it comes into language, but language, too, has its real being only in the fact that the world is presented in it" (TM, 443). It is language, Gadamer explains, that allows us a certain distance from the embededness in the environment that other animals experience. Language provides a certain space from this environment so that we are able to have a *view* of it, have an *orientation* with regard to it, and have a *relationship* with it *as a world* (a view, an orientation, and a relation that emerge in our activity of talking about something). Our language opens up for us a world filled with relationships that constitute the significance of its various parts. Our language gives us or, more properly, *is* our worldview. In rising above the environment, by bringing it into language as a world or worldview, the human being achieves for itself a freedom that the other animals do not experience—a freedom that allows us to foreground, present, delineate, and describe the various subject matter of our world, imagine things in different combinations, and (most important for Gadamer) *ask about things*, which opens us to the inquiry in which there is the possibility of coming to grasp truths. We cannot ignore, here, that this is all accomplished from Gadamer's point of view in an explicit linguistic mode that involves putting the subject matter into words.

Gadamer's point, here, seems to be that if I have some experience in the world in which I understand something without immediately articulating it verbally, this understanding not only (a) is parasitic on language, in that it is made possible because of the language in which things already have a meaningful place in my world, and a significant relationship to me; but also (b) must be speakable in words. In other words, it must be possible— though perhaps with great difficulty—to give an account of any experience I have, and it is in such an account that the experience becomes fully intelligible. Perhaps, for instance, I finally "get" what some painting is trying to communicate, or perhaps I finally learn to follow the movements of my modern dance teacher, which initially seemed chaotic and impossible. Perhaps I teach myself to ski or I learn to play a musical instrument by ear. From Gadamer's point of view, these experiences themselves begin because "painting," "dance," "teacher," "snow," "ski," "music," and "instrument" are all meaningful parts of my world, and I am already related to them through language. I approach all of them *as something* before my further experience begins. But, furthermore, the experiences I have with them really only become fully intelligible when they are put into words, which constitutes for Gadamer the real medium in which anything is truly understood (for, as he has formulated it, "being that can be understood is language").[1] So, in the case that I (after learning to play my musical instrument) display my interpretive understanding of a famous song in my performance of it, my unique interpretation must be speakable—even if this process of verbalization is an open-ended, inexhaustible process. Gadamer states: "A performing artist may feel that justifying his interpretation in words is very secondary, rejecting it as inartistic, but he cannot want to deny that such an account can be given of his reproductive interpretation . . . and this interpretation will take place in verbal form" (TM, 399–400). It is in this verbal interpretation, as Gadamer sees it, that understanding is really fulfilled.

It is when understanding is raised to "the word" and made explicit that it reaches its *full* realization and concretion: "the word is that in which knowledge is consummated" (TM, 426). True knowledge for Gadamer, then, is seen in the Socratic spirit as something that only takes place in its *most genuine form* in the process of giving an account of some subject matter in language—in "the movement of dialogue, in which word and idea first become what they are" (TM, xxxvii).

NONVERBAL PLAY: ARROWS AND OPENERS

An explicit understanding in words, then, remains a real possibility and potential for us, but it is also a possibility and potential that can be blocked. When we find parties unwilling to engage with each other in the explicit sense of a literal speaking and being spoken to, we need a direction in which to turn that offers us an alternative to the-all-too popular tendencies of disengagement or force, which have a destructive effect on the play-movement that constitutes our human form of life, and the motion of life in general. We need to look to other forms of engagement or, as I would like to suggest, nonverbal forms of play (which may very well be parasitic on a previous learning of language, even if it is not *explicitly* used) to find those games that have the power of opening us to the verbal dialogue in which the highest levels of understanding and self-understanding can be achieved.

Following Gadamer's lead, and appropriating his insight regarding the importance of preserving the movement of play for life, it is our turn to take on the role of the phenomenologist and to seek out those events of play in which we experience an opening to dialogue. In seeking out such nonverbal games, I find myself continually returning to a form of engage-ment that Gadamer has barely mentioned at all: sport. Peoples of the most varied ideological, political, and religious convictions—people who may even be completely opposed on most issues, and might be "at war" (in the "hot" or "cold" sense of the word) with each other—find themselves willing and even *eager* to engage in the competitive games of sport. There is something about this particular family of games that offers us a space of back-and-forth engagement even when dialogue has broken down and has, as I would like to suggest, the power of re-opening conversation.[2]

Of course, the motivation behind the eagerness to engage in this type of play usually amounts to a profound desire to dominate one's opponent in competition and prove one's superiority on a public stage. But despite this "spirit of competitiveness" with which parties may enter into such games, the process of the game itself seems to have a surprising effect on players and their orientation toward each other, even in spite of their prejudgments toward one another and their single intent of "winning." Something happens to them over and above their wanting and trying (to appropriate a Gadamerian way of expressing the phenomenon of play). In devoting all their resources, energy, and skill to "outplay" their competi-tor throughout the game, parties that are intent on beating a "rival" or "arch enemy" find themselves confronting what begins to increasingly appear as a "worthy opponent," and even developing respect where there previously was none. This seed of respect becomes a first stage in a process of opening, for it leads to "the question"—the question, perhaps asked first only to oneself—of how one's competitor is playing so well. What is his strategy? What are his training techniques? How does he do what he does? The recognition occurs, again as if in spite of oneself, that one's competitor knows something of significance that is worth learning. As we have seen, the question is the crucial moment of simultaneously breaking open the subject matter and sparking the movement of dialogue, and it rests on the recognition that one's partner is able to contribute insight beyond one's own regarding the subject matter at hand.

We can observe, further, that not only does the game of sport have the power to open its players to a new respect for each other, which pulls participants toward dialogue, but it also has the power to open its spectators to a new recognition of the competitors' abilities and knowl-edge. As Gadamer has shown us, the spectator becomes a participant and player in the game itself, and in becoming caught up in the competition playing out before him, the spectator too finds his prejudgments being challenged and transformed. We have watched the way the Olympic Games have been an ongoing arena in which racist and sexist prejudices have been tested and transformed for the world, and not only for those individuals competing. There is a way in which strong competitors, regardless of who they might be and what prejudgments we might have of them, make a claim on us that demands our recognition—and without the explicit word. But we have seen that this *recognition of an ability and knowledge beyond our own* is the condition for the possibility of an opening to genuine dialogue.

The competitive game of sport is promising as a type of play that can encourage an opening to dialogue for another important reason. Because every sport operates within the bounds of a set of rules, which must be agreed upon and followed by the players if the game is to function, sport offers players a special opportunity to show their opponents that they are willing to "play fair." It may be that the players are only willing to play fair because they don't want there to be any question about whether they've dominated their opponent legitimately through sheer strength and skill. But regardless of the ultimate motivation behind fair play, sport is an opportunity to cultivate an initial level of trust between opponents who are too guarded for dialogue. It is this cultivation of trust that can inspire an opening to types of engagement, like dialogue, that require even more trust.

I am encouraged by the growing interest in sport as a phenomenon that is worthy of philosophical reflection. Drew Hyland is surely correct in his book *Philosophy of Sport* when he declares that there has been a long prejudice in academia that the topic of sport, as well as that of play, is surely not profound or serious enough to warrant much reflective attention, no matter how central a role it may play in our culture. But against such a prejudice, he invites us to consider how we, in and through the phenomenon of sport (just as we saw with the phenomenon of play) come to a greater self-knowledge, become aware of our own finitude, develop self-discipline, learn how to participate with others (as part of a team), and cultivate in ourselves a heightened "responsive-openness" in what Hyland calls the "stance of sport."[3] Considering (a) that these aspects are all internal to the game of dialogical understanding, which Gadamer has shown us is so crucial for the enrichment of our human form of life, and considering (b) the central place that sport holds in such a wide variety of cultures, where we find a widespread eagerness to take part in the game, it seems that the game of sport is not a bad place to start when we are looking for a kind of engagement that can encourage the type of I-Thou relations necessary for dialogue.

Competitive sport is, here, offered as just one example of the kind of nonverbal game that has the power to open its participants to dialogue where they previously found themselves closed. There are a number of other competitive games that, for the same reasons as sport, would also have the power to open participants to dialogue. Though they may not seem like competitive games at first glance, research and discovery (in the natural and historical sciences), exploration (of land, space, and sea), and achievement in the arts and in technological innovation regularly become competitive games between players, or opponents, who want nothing more than to prove their superior intellect or ability. These activities can engage opponents in a kind of "race" that does not require them to converse, but at the same time encourages the curiosity and interest in each other's knowledge that can lead to respect and dialogue. In addition to competitive games, exchange games like trade are also promising modes of interaction that have the power to open players to dialogue. Like sport, trade is one of those forms of engagement that even those who are unwilling to interact on any other level still seem willing and even eager to begin and sustain. We find that even those who carry the attitude that they would rather avoid each other (or fight each other), rather than converse, are still motivated to exchange goods, information, or natural resources out of need. The game of trade, inspired by mutual need and serving the mutual benefit of the players, has the power to cultivate in players a recognition of overlapping interests. Overlapping interests, in turn, provide both the motivation for dialogue (since both parties will need deeper cooperation if they are to fulfill their needs) and the shared subject matter about which to talk.

These examples of competitive games and exchange games, as types of nonverbal play that have the power to open us to dialogue, are preliminary suggestions, arrows, and openers that call for further contribution. In the spirit of dialogic play, they are what we might call a "good will" offering—an attempt to think along with Gadamer philosophically, phenomenologically, and ethically, and to apply what rings true in Gadamer's work to contemporary problems facing us. With this contribution, I hope to join Gadamer in an effort to cultivate the conditions for the dialogic play in which our human understanding, and human form of life, approaches its highest potential.

Ongoing dialogue, where human beings are related in "openness" to each other and to the truths they are coming to grasp, represents for Gadamer the unending "conversation that we ourselves are" (TM, 378). This phrase expresses our mode of being-in-the-world as understanding, and also emphasizes that we cannot conceive of knowledge as something that is ultimately private, personal, or monological. It is not something we have or develop by ourselves. It is, rather, communal and, thus, cannot be detached from our relations with other human beings. It also cannot be detached from the manner in which we choose to relate to one another. It cannot be detached from ethics. The "conversation that we are" can surely take a genuine or less than genuine, flourishing or degenerating, engaged or rather disengaged form. Philosophical Hermeneutics, as a practical philosophy, offers us ethical guidance past a variety of obstacles to genuine dialogue that willing interlocutors tend to set for themselves. But where Gadamer's guiding "ethics of play" limits itself to scenarios in which there already exists "friendly" I-Thou relations, some of the hardest questions of ethics that we face in our era—in particular, the question of how we are to engage our not-so-friendly "Other"—remain neglected. *Our* ethics of play, *our* phenomenological and practical task, then, takes us beyond dialogic play in search of other forms of play-engagement in which an opening to dialogue can be achieved. In taking up this new challenge, we join Gadamer in the effort to cultivate the conditions for genuine dialogue and understanding in which we grow and flourish as a human community.

NOTES

1. This, I will admit, is one of the most difficult aspects of Gadamer's philosophy to follow. I cannot help but sense that there is a certain forgetting of the body and its ability to learn through pure spontaneity, experimentation, repetition, and practice.

2. One interesting historical example of this phenomenon was the way in which China and America finally re-opened to dialogue after more than twenty years of cold silence. What sparked a new age of engagement between the countries was none other than a ping-pong tournament. In 1971, the U.S. ping-pong team was the first group of Americans allowed into China since 1949, beginning an era of what was termed "ping-pong diplomacy" (in which the Chinese team toured the United States to play "Friendship First" matches), and which led to a visit by Nixon to Beijing, where explicit talks and negotiations between the countries were able to begin.

3. Drew Hyland, *Philosophy of Sport* (St. Paul: Paragon House, 1990), 125–46.

Bibliography

Aristotle. *Nicomachean Ethics*. Translated by Martin Ostwald. New York: Macmillan Publishing Co., 1962.

Bernasconi, Robert. "You Don't Know What I'm Talking About: Alterity and the Hermeneutical Ideal." In *The Specter of Relativism*, edited by Lawrence Schmidt, 178–94. Evanston: Northwestern University Press, 1995.

Bernstein, Richard J. *Beyond Objectivism and Relativism: Science Hermeneutics and Praxis*. Philadelphia: University of Pennsylvania Press, 1983.

———. "The Constellation of Hermeneutics, Critical Theory and Deconstruction." In *The Cambridge Companion to Gadamer*, edited by Robert J. Dostal, 267–82. Cambridge: Cambridge University Press, 2002.

———. *The New Constellation: The Ethical-Political Horizons of Modernity/Postmodernity*. Cambridge: MIT Press, 1991.

———. *Philosophical Profiles: Essays in a Pragmatic Mode*. Philadelphia: University of Pennsylvania Press, 1986.

Betti, Emilio. "Hermeneutics as the General Methodology of the *Geisteswissenschaften*." In *Contemporary Hermeneutics: Hermeneutics as Method, Philosophy and Critique*, translated by Joseph Bleicher. London and New York: Routledge & Kegan Paul, 1980.

Bleicher, Joseph. *Contemporary Hermeneutics: Hermeneutics as Method, Philosophy and Critique*. London and New York: Routledge and Kegan Paul, 1980.

Buber, Martin. *I and Thou*. Translated by Walter Kaufmann. New York: Touchstone, 1970.

Caputo, John D. *Radical Hermeneutics: Repetition, Deconstruction and the Hermeneutic Project*. Bloomington and Indianapolis: Indiana University Press, 1987.

Descartes, René. *Mediations on First Philosophy*. Translated by John Cottingham. Cambridge: Cambridge University Press, 1986.

Dilthey, Wilhelm. "The Rise of Hermeneutics." In *The Hermeneutic Tradition: From Ast to Ricouer*, edited by Gayle L. Ormiston and Alan D. Schrift, 101–14. Albany: SUNY Press, 1990.

Dostal, Robert J., ed. *The Cambridge Companion to Gadamer*. Cambridge: Cambridge University Press, 2002.

Gadamer, Hans-Georg. *Dialogue and Dialectic: Eight Hermeneutical Studies on Plato*. Translated and edited by P. Christopher Smith. New Haven, Conn.: Yale University Press, 1980.

———. "Hermeneutics and Social Science." *Cultural Hermeneutics* 2 (1975): 307–16.

———. *Hermeneutics, Religion, and Ethics*. Translated by J. Weinsheimer. New Haven, Conn.: Yale University Press, 1999.

———. *The Idea of the Good in Platonic-Aristotelian Philosophy*. Translated by P. Christopher Smith. New Haven, Conn.: Yale University Press, 1986.

———. *Philosophical Hermeneutics*. Translated and edited by David E. Linge. Berkeley and Los Angeles: University of California Press, 1976.

———. *Plato's Dialectical Ethics: Phenomenological Interpretations Relating to the Philebus*. Translated and edited by Robert M. Wallace. New Haven, Conn.: Yale University Press, 1991.

———. *Praise of Theory: Speeches and Essays*. Translated by Chris Dawson. New Haven and London: Yale University Press, 1998.

———. *Reason in the Age of Science*. Translated by Frederick G. Lawrence. Cambridge: MIT Press, 1981.

————. *The Relevance of the Beautiful and Other Essays*. Translated by Nicholas Walker, edited by Robert Bernasconi. Cambridge: Cambridge University Press, 1986.

————. *Truth and Method*. Translated by J. Weinsheimer and Donald G. Marshall. 2nd revised edition. New York: Continuum, 2000.

————. *Wahrheit und Methode: Grundzüge einer philosophischen Hermeneutik*. 6th edition. Tübingen: J.C.B. Mohr, 1990.

Grondin, Jean. *Introduction to Philosophical Hermeneutics*. Translated by Joel Weinsheimer. New Haven and London: Yale University Press, 1994.

Habermas, Jürgen. "A Review of Gadamer's *Truth and Method*." Translated by Fred Dallmayr and Thomas McCarthy. In *The Hermeneutic Tradition: From Ast to Ricouer*, edited by Gayle L. Ormiston and Alan D. Schrift, 213–44. Albany: SUNY Press, 1990.

————. "The Hermeneutic Claim to Universality." Translated by Josef Bleicher. In *The Hermeneutic Tradition: From Ast to Ricouer*, edited by Gayle L. Ormiston and Alan D. Schrift, 245–72. Albany: SUNY Press, 1990.

————. *Knowledge and Human Interests*. Translated by Jeremy J. Shapiro. Boston: Beacon Press, 1971.

Hegel, G. W. F. *Phenomenology of Sprit*. Translated by A. V. Miller. Oxford: Oxford University Press, 1977.

Heidegger, Martin. *Being and Time*. Translated by John Macquarrie and Edward Robinson. New York: Harper & Row Publishers, 1962.

Hahn, Lewis Edwin, ed. *The Philosophy of Hans-Georg Gadamer*. The Library of Living Philosophers XXIV. Chicago and LaSalle: Open Court, 1997.

Hirsch, E. D. *Validity in Interpretation*. New Haven and London: Yale University Press, 1967.

Hyland, Drew. *Philosophy of Sport*. St. Paul, Minn.: Paragon House, 1990.

————. *The Question of Play*. Lanham, Md.: University Press of America, 1984.

Michelfelder, Diane and Richard Palmer, eds. *Dialogue and Deconstruction: The Gadamer-Derrida Encounter*. Albany: SUNY Press, 1989.

Misgeld, Dieter and Graeme Nicholson, eds. *Hans-Georg Gadamer on Education, Poetry, and History: Applied Hermeneutics*. Albany: SUNY Press, 1992.

Ormiston, Gayle L. and Alan D. Schrift, eds. *The Hermeneutic Tradition*. Albany: SUNY Press, 1990.

Palmer, Richard E. *Hermeneutics: Interpretation Theory in Schleiermacher, Dilthey, Heidegger, and Gadamer*. Evanston, Ill.: Northwestern University Press, 1969.

Plato. *Early Socratic Dialogues*. Edited by Trevor J. Saunders. London: Penguin Books, 1987.

————. *Five Dialogues. Euthyphro, Apology, Crito, Meno, Phaedo*. Translated by G. M. A. Grube. Indianapolis and Cambridge: Hackett, 1981.

————. *The Republic of Plato*. Translated by Allan Bloom. Basic Books, 1968.

————. *The Symposium and The Phaedrus: Plato's Erotic Dialogues*. Translated by William Cobb. Albany: SUNY Press, 1993.

Risser, James. *Hermeneutics and the Voice of the Other: Re-reading Gadamer's Philosophical Hermeneutics*. Albany: SUNY Press, 1997.

Schmidt, Lawrence K., ed. *Language and Linguisticality*. Lanham, Md.: Lexington Books, 2000.

————. "Respecting Others: The Hermeneutic Virtue." *Continental Philosophy Review* 33, no. 3 (July 2000): 359–79.

————. *The Specter of Relativism: Truth, Dialogue, and Phronesis in Philosophical Hermeneutics*. Evanston, Ill.: Northwestern University Press, 1995.

Seeskin, Kenneth. *Dialogue and Discovery: A Study in Socratic Method*. Albany: SUNY Press, 1987.

Smith, P. Christopher. *Hermeneutics and Human Finitude: Toward a Theory of Ethical Understanding*. New York: Fordham Press, 1991.

Warnke, Georgia. *Gadamer: Hermeneutics, Tradition and Reason*. Stanford, Calif.: Stanford University Press, 1987.

Wright, Kathleen, ed. *Festivals of Interpretation: Essays on Hans-Georg Gadamer's Work.* Albany: SUNY Press, 1990.

Index

153

historische Gerechtigkeit (historical
impartiality), 13; von Ranke on, 13
historische Weltanschauung (historical
worldview), 12–13
history: effective, 19; grasp of, 14; as
ongoing process, 14; teleological
view of, 12–13
horizon (*Horizont*), 25; as background,
52; as changeable, 85–86; as concept,
69; fusion of, 55–63; openness of,
85–86; of present, 56
Horizontverschmelzung (fusion of
horizons), 50–51; Betti on, 60, 61–62;
requirements for, 62–63;
understanding and, 60–61
human condition, 11, 14
human finitude, 18–19; openness and,
85–86
humanism, 20
human play, 34–36, 46; freedom and, 34
human rationality, 65–66
human sciences (*Geisteswissenschaften*),
3–4, 5–15, 20; natural sciences v.,
5–8; as whole, 44
human scientist, natural scientist v., 7
Hyland, Drew, 46, 146

Ich und Du. See I/Thou
I/It dichotomy, 26–27
imitation (*mimesis*), 40–41; meaning of,
47
individual life-experiences, 14–15
individual potential, 139–140
Ineinanderspiel (interplay), 57, 63
in/out dichotomy, 26–27
insights, 4
integration, 69
intelligence (*nous*), 122
interlocutors, 102–103; play of, 67–69;
relationship of, 108
interplay (*Ineinanderspiel*), 57, 63
interpretation (*Auslegung*), 19, 56,
63–64; definition of, 141–142;
engaged, 54; incorrect, 57; of
language, 140; of picture, 43; seeing
and, 17; task of, 53–54;
theory/practice of, 3; verbal form of,
143–144
interpreting being, 4

I/Thou, 67, 68–69, 136; relationship of,
75–76, 78–79, 94

Kant, Immanuel, 13; on aesthetic
beauty, 21; Cartesian world view
and, 29; ethics of, 94; on knowledge,
21; on taste, 46
knowledge: Aristotle and, 121–124;
deformation of, 118; edifice of, 27;
genuine, 19, 25; Kant on, 21; mode
of, 8, 20, 41; modern scientific notion
of, IV.5–IV.8, 4, 5; objective, 8, 13, 28;
practical, 121–124; pure, 121–122; as
representation, 27; restriction of, 46;
of self, 71; of spirit, 71; of truth, 37; of
world, 29
Kommunikationspartner (genuine
partner in dialogue), 76. See also
dialogue
Kunst (art), 9

language: definition of, 143–144;
explicit, 143; as game, 68–69;
interpretation of, 140; as medium,
142; for Schleiermacher, 81; as term,
140–141; as tool, 68; tradition as, 67;
words and, 140–144
law, 119–120
Leben (life), 9
Lebensäußerung (expression of life), 78
life, 9; human form of, 137
linguisticality (*Sprachlichkeit*), 141
literary form, differences in, 45–46
literature: as borderline, 45;
understanding of, 44–46
lived experience. See experience

master, active, 7
meaning(s), 4; anticipation of, 57;
common, 8; communication of, 6–7;
conception of, 62; context of, 6;
grasping, 5–6; understanding of, 15
meaningful whole (*Sinnganze*), 36;
projection of, 51
mediation (*Vermittlung*): as concept, 47;
historical, 70; between past/present,
50–51
mediational epistemology, 29
merging, 58

About the Author

Monica Vilhauer is assistant professor of philosophy at Roanoke College. She earned her Ph.D. in philosophy from the New School for Social Research in New York, NY. Her teaching and research interests include ethics, nineteenth- and twentieth-century continental philosophy, ancient philosophy, and feminist philosophy. She is secretary for the North American Society for Philosophical Hermeneutics (NASPH) and she is co-creator and coordinator of the Gender & Women's Studies Concentration at Roanoke College.